TRISTRAM

THE MACMILLAN COMPANY
NEW YORK • CHICAGO
DALLAS • ATLANTA • SAN FRANCISCO
LONDON • MANILA

IN CANADA
BRETT-MACMILLAN LTD.
GALT, ONTARIO

TRISTRAM

BY

EDWIN ARLINGTON ROBINSON

New York

THE MACMILLAN COMPANY

1960

TO

THE MEMORY OF

EDWARD PROBY FOX

TRISTRAM

TRISTRAM

I

Isolt of the white hands, in Brittany,
Could see no longer northward anywhere
A picture more alive or less familiar
Than a blank ocean and the same white birds
Flying, and always flying, and still flying,
Yet never bringing any news of him
That she remembered, who had sailed away
The spring before—saying he would come back,
Although not saying when.   Not one of them,
For all their flying, she thought, had heard the name
Of Tristram, or of him beside her there
That was the King, her father.   The last ship
Was out of sight, and there was nothing now
For her to see before the night came down
Except her father's face.   She looked at him
And found him smiling in the way she feared,

And loved the while she feared it.   The King took
One of her small still hands in one of his
That were so large and hard to be so kind,
And weighed a question. not for the first time:

"Why should it be that I must have a child
Whose eyes are wandering always to the north?
The north is a bad region full of wolves
And bears and hairy men that have no manners.
Why should her eyes be always on the north,
I wonder, when all's here that one requires
Of comfort, love, and of expediency?
You are not cheered, I see, or satisfied
Entirely by the sound of what I say.
You are too young, may be, to make yourself
A nest of comfort and expediency."

"I may be that," she said, and a quick flush
Made a pink forage of her laughing face,
At which he smiled again.   "But not so young
As to be told for ever how young I am.
I have been growing for these eighteen years,
And waiting here, for one thing and another.

Besides, his manners are as good as yours,
And he's not half so hairy as you are,
Even though you be the King of Brittany,
Or the great Jove himself, and then my father."
With that she threw her arms around his neck,
Throbbing as if she were a child indeed.

"You are no heavier than a cat," said he,
"But otherwise you are somewhat like a tiger
Relinquish your commendable affection
A little, and tell me why it is you dream
Of someone coming always from the north.
Are there no proper knights or princes else
Than one whose eyes, wherever they may be fixed,
Are surely not fixed hard on Brittany?
You are a sort of child, or many sorts,
Yet also are too high and too essential
To be much longer the quaint sport and food
Of shadowy fancies. For a time I've laughed
And let you dream, but I may not laugh always,
Because he praised you as a child one day,
And may have liked you as a child one day.
Why do you stare for ever into the north,

Over that water, where the good God placed
A land known only to your small white ears?"

"Only because the good God, I suppose,
Placed England somewhere north of Brittany—
Though not so far but one may come and go
As many a time as twice before he dies.
I know that's true, having been told about it.
I have been told so much about this world
That I have wondered why men stay in it.
I have been told of devils that are in it,
And some right here in Brittany. Griffon
Is one of them; and if he ever gets me,
I'll pray for the best way to kill myself."

King Howel held his daughter closer to him,
As if a buried and forgotten fear
Had come to life and was confronting him
With a new face. "Never you mind the devils,"
He said, "be they in Brittany or elsewhere.
They are for my attention, if need be.
You will affright me and amuse me less
By saying, if you are ready, how much longer

You are to starve yourself with your delusion
Of Tristram coming back. He may come back,
Or Mark, his uncle, who tonight is making
Another Isolt his queen—the dark Isolt,
Isolt of Ireland—may be coming back,
Though I'd as lief he would remain at home
In Cornwall, with his new queen—if he keeps her."

"And who is this far-off Isolt of Ireland?"
She said, like a thing waiting to be hurt:
"A creature that one hears of constantly,
And one that no man sees, or none to say so,
Must be unusual—if she be at all."

"The few men who have told of her to me
Have told of silence and of Irish pride,
Inhabiting too much beauty for one woman.
My eyes have never seen her; and as for beauty,
My eyes would rather look on yours, my child.
And as for Tristram coming back, what then—
One of these days? Any one may come back.
King Arthur may come back; and as for that,
Our Lord and Saviour may come back some time,

Though hardly all for you. Have you kept hid
Some promise or protestation heretofore,
That you may shape a thought into a reason
For making always of a distant wish
A dim belief? You are too old for that—
If it will make you happy to be told so.
You have been told so much." King Howel smiled,
And waited. holding her white hands in his.

"I have been told that Tristram will come back,"
She said; "and it was he who told me so.
Also I have this agate that he gave me;
And I believe his eyes."

                              "Believe his agate,"
The king said, "for as long as you may save it.
An agate's a fair plaything for a child,
Though not so boundless and immovable
In magnitude but that a child may lose it.
Since you esteem it such an acquisition,
Treasure it more securely, and believe it
As a bright piece of earth, and nothing more.
Believe his agate, and forget his eyes;

And go to bed. You are not young enough,
I see, to stay awake and entertain
Much longer your exaggerated fancies.
And if he should come back? Would you prepare
Upon the ruinous day of his departure
To drown yourself, and with yourself his agate?"

Isolt, now on a cushion at his feet,
Finding the King's hard knees a meagre pillow,
Sat upright, thinking. "No I should not do that;
Though I should never trust another man
So far that I should go away with him.
King's daughters, I suppose, are bought and sold,
But you would not sell me."

                            "You seize a question
As if it were an agate—or a fact,"
The King said, laughing at the calm gray eyes
That were so large in the small face before him.
"I might sell you, perhaps, at a fair bargain.
To play with an illustrious example,
If Modred were to overthrow King Arthur—
And there are prophets who see Arthur's end
In Modred, who's an able sort of reptile—

And come for you to go away with him,
And to be Queen of Britain, I might sell you,
Perhaps.   You might say prayers that you be sold."

"I may say prayers that you be reasonable
And serious, and that you believe me so."
There was a light now in his daughter's eyes
Like none that he remembered having seen
In eyes before, whereat he paused and heard,
Not all amused.   "He will come back," she said,
"And I shall wait.   If he should not come back,
I shall have been but one poor woman more
Whose punishment for being born a woman
Was to believe and wait.   You are my King,
My father, and of all men anywhere,
Save one, you are the world of men to me.
When I say this of him you must believe me,
As I believe his eyes.   He will come back;
And what comes then I leave to him, and God."

Slowly the King arose, and with his hands
He lifted up Isolt, so frail, so light,
And yet, with all, mysteriously so strong.
He raised her patient face between his hands,

Observing it as if it were some white
And foreign flower, not certain in his garden
To thrive, nor like to die.   Then with a vague
And wavering effect of shaking her
Affectionately back to his own world,
Which never would be hers, he smiled once more
And set her free.   "You should have gone to bed
When first I told you.   You had best go now,
And while you are still dreaming.   In the morning
Your dreams, if you remember them, will all
Be less than one bird singing in a tree."

Isolt of the white hands, unchangeable,
Half childlike and half womanly, looked up
Into her father's eyes and shook her head,
Smiling, but less for joy than certainty:
"There's a bird then that I have never seen
In Brittany; and I have never heard him.
Good night, my father."   She went slowly out,
Leaving him in the gloom.

                      "Good night, my child
Good night," he said, scarce hearing his own voice
For crowded thoughts that were unseizable

And unforeseen within him.   Like Isolt,
He stood now in the window looking north
Over the misty sea.   A seven days' moon
Was in the sky, and there were a few stars
That had no fire.   "I have no more a child,"
He thought, "and what she is I do not know.
It may be fancy and fantastic youth
That ails her now; it may be the sick touch
Of prophecy concealing disillusion.
If there were not inwoven so much power
And poise of sense with all her seeming folly,
I might assume a concord with her faith
As that of one elected soon to die.
But surely no infringement of the grave
In her conceits and her appearances
Encourages a fear that still is fear;
And what she is to know, I cannot say.
A changeling down from one of those white stars
Were more like her than like a child of mine."

Nothing in the cold glimmer of a moon
Over a still, cold ocean there before him
Would answer for him in the silent voice

Of time an idle question. So the King,
With only time for company, stood waiting
Alone there in the window, looking off
At the still sea between his eyes and England.

II

The moon that glimmered cold on Brittany
Glimmered as cold on Cornwall, where King **Mark,**
Only by kingly circumstance endowed
With friends enough to make a festival,
On this dim night had married and made **Queen—**
Of all fair women in the world by fate
The most forgotten in her loveliness
Till now—Isolt of Ireland, who had flamed
And fought so long with love that she called hate,
Inimical to Tristram for the stroke
That felled Morhaus her kinsman. Tristram, **blind**
With angry beauty, or in honor blind,
Or in obscure obedience unawakened,
Had given his insane promise to his uncle
Of intercession with the Irish King
And so drawn out of him a slow assent,
Not fathoming or distinguishing aright
[19]

Within himself a passion that was death,
Nor gauging with a timely recognition
The warfare of a woman's enmity
With love without love's name. He knew too late
How one word then would have made arras-rats
For her of all his uncles, and all kings
That he might serve with cloudy promises,
Not weighed until redeemed. Now there was time
For him to weigh them, and to weigh them well,
To the last scorching ounce of desperation,
Searing his wits and flesh like heated mail
Amidst the fiery downfall of a palace,
Where there was no one left except himself
To save, and no way out except through fire.

Partly to balk his rage, partly to curse
Unhindered an abject ineptitude
That like a drug had held him and withheld him
In seizing once from love's imperial garden
The flower of all things there, now Tristram leaned
Alone upon a parapet below
The lights of high Tintagel, where gay music
Had whipped him as a lash and driven him out

Into the misty night, which might have held
A premonition and a probing chill
For one more tranquil and less exigent,
And not so much on fire.   Down through the gloom
He gazed at nothing, save a moving blur
Where foamed eternally on Cornish rocks
The moan of Cornish water; and he asked,
With a malignant inward voice of envy,
How many scarred cold things that once had laughed
And loved and wept and sung, and had been men,
Might have been knocked and washed indifferently
On that hard shore, and eaten gradually
By competent quick fishes and large crabs
And larger birds, not caring a wink which
Might be employed on their spent images,
No longer tortured there, if God was good,
By memories of the fools and royal pimps
That once unwittingly they might have been—
Like Tristram, who could wish himself as far
As they were from a wearing out of life
On a racked length of days.   Now and again
A louder fanfare of malicious horns
Would sing down from the festival above him,

Smiting his angry face like a wet clout
That some invisible scullion might have swung,
Too shadowy and too agile to be seized
And flung down on those rocks.   Now and again
Came over him a cold soul-retching wave
Of recognition past reality,
Recurrent, vile, and always culminating
In a forbidden vision thrice unholy
Of Mark, his uncle, like a man-shaped goat
Appraising with a small salacious eye,
And slowly forcing into his gaunt arms,
And all now in a few impossible hours
That were as possible as pain and death,
The shuddering unreal miracle of Isolt,
Which was as real as torture to the damned
In hell, or in Cornwall.   Before long now
That music and that wordless murmuring
Of distant men and women, who divined
As much or little as they might, would cease;
The mocking lights above him would go out;
There would be silence; and the King would hold
Isolt—Isolt of the dark eyes—Isolt
Of the patrician passionate helplessness—

Isolt of the soft waving blue-black hair—
Isolt of Ireland—in his vicious arms
And crush the bloom of her resisting life
On his hot, watery mouth, and overcome
The protest of her suffering silk skin
With his crude senile claws. And it was he,
Tristram, the loud-accredited strong warrior,
Tristram, the loved of women, the harp-player,
Tristram, the learned Nimrod among hunters,
Tristram, the most obedient imbecile
And humble servant of King Mark his uncle,
Who had achieved all this. For lack of sight
And sense of self, and imperturbably,
He had achieved all this and might do more,
No doubt, if given the time. Whereat he cursed
Himself again, and his complacent years
Of easy blindness. Time had saved for him
The flower that he had not the wit to seize
And carry a few leagues across the water,
Till when he did so it was his no more,
And body and soul were sick to think of it.
Why should he not be sick? "Good God in heaven,"
He groaned aloud, "why should I not be sick!"

"No God will answer you to say why not,"
Said one descending heavily but unheard,
And slowly, down the stairs. "And one like me,
Having seen more seasons out than you have seen,
Would say it was tonight your prime intention
To make yourself the sickest man in Cornwall."
Gouvernail frowned and shivered as he spoke,
And waited as a stranger waits in vain
Outside a door that none within will open.

"I may be that already," Tristram said,
"But I'm not cold. For I'm a seer tonight,
And consequently full of starry thoughts.
The stars are not so numerous as they were,
But there's a brotherly white moon up there,
Such as it is. Well, Gouvernail, what word
Has my illustrious and most amorous
And most imperious Uncle Mark prepared
For you to say to me that you come scowling
So far down here to say it? You are next
To nearest, not being my father, of all men
Of whom I am unworthy. What's the word?"

"Tristram, I left the King annoyed and anxious
On your account, and for the nonce not pleased."

"What most annoys my uncle, for the nonce?
God knows that I have done for him of late
More than an army, made of nephews only,
Shall ever be fools enough to do again.
When tired of feasting and of too much talk,
And too much wine and too much happy music,
May not his royal nephew have some air,
Even though his annoyed uncle be a king?
My father is a king, in Lyonesse;
And that's about as much as being a king
In Cornwall is—or one here now might say so."

"Forgive me Tristram, but I'm old for this.
The King knows well what you have done for him,
And owns a gratitude beyond the gift
Of utterance for the service of your word.
But the King does not know, and cannot know,
Your purpose in an act ungenerous,
If not unseemly. What shall I say to him
If I go back to him alone? Tristram,
There are some treasured moments I remember
When you have made me loyal to you always
For saying good words of me, and with no care

Whether or not they came back to my ears.
Surely, if past attention and tuition
Are not forgotten, you will not forget
This present emptiness of my confusion.
If I go back alone, what shall I say?"

"Say to the King that if the King command
Implacably my presence, I will come.
But say as an addition that I'm sick,
And that another joyful hour with him
This night might have eventful influences.
Nothing could be more courteous, if said well,
Or more consistent with infirm allegiance.
Say to the King I'm sick. If he doubts that,
Or takes it ill, say to the King I'm drunk.
His comprehensions and remembrances
Will compass and envisage, peradventure,
The last deplorable profundity
Of my defection if you say, for me,
That in my joy my caution crept away
Like an unfaithful hound and went to sleep.
Gouvernail, you are cold."

                                    Gouvernail sighed
And fixed an eye calm with experience,

And with affection kind, on Tristram, sadly.
"Yes, I am cold," he said. "Here at my heart
I feel a blasting chill. Will you not come
With me to see the King and Queen together?
Or must I mumble as I may to them,
Alone, this weary jest of your complaint?"

"God's love, have I not seen the two together!
And as for my complaint, mumble or not.
Mumble or shriek it; or, as you see fit,
Call for my harp and sing it." Tristram laid
His hands on Gouvernail's enduring shoulders
Which many a time had carried him for sport
In a far vanished childhood, and looked off
Where patient skill had made of shrubs and rocks
Together a wild garden half way down
To the dusk-hidden shore. "Believe my word,
My loyal and observing Gouvernail,"
He said, and met the older man's regard
With all that he could muster of a smile.
"Believe my word, and say what I have said,
Or something as much better as you may.
Believe my word no less that I am sick,

And that I'd feed a sick toad to my brother
If in my place he were not sick without it."

Gouvernail sighed, and with a deeper sigh
Looked off across the sea. "Tristram," he said,
"I can see no good coming out of this,
But I will give your message as I can,
And with as light misgiving as I may.
Yet where there is no love, too often I find
As perilous a constriction in our judgment
As where there is too much."

                              Tristram pursued
The mentor of his childhood and his youth
With no more words, and only made of him
In the returning toil of his departure
A climbing silence that would soon be met
By sound and light, and by King Mark again,
And by Isolt again. Isolt of Ireland!
Isolt, so soon to be the bartered prey
Of an unholy sacrifice, by rites
Of Rome made holy. Tristram groaned and wept,
And heard once more the changeless moan below

Of an insensate ocean on those rocks
Whereon he had a mind to throw himself.
"My God! If I were dreaming this," he said,
"My sleep would be a penance for a year.
But I am neither dead nor dreaming now,
I'm living and awake. If this be life,
What a soul-healing difference death must be,
Being something else . . . Isolt! Isolt of Ireland!"

Gazing at emptiness for a long time
He looked away from life, and scarcely heard,
Coming down slowly towards him from above,
A troubling sound of cloth. "Good evening, sir,
Perhaps you do not know me, or remember
That once you gave a lady so much honor
As to acknowledge her obscure existence.
From late accounts you are not here to know
Your friends on this especial famous evening.
Why do you stay away from history
Like this? Kings are not married every night."

Perceiving there beside him a slim figure
Provisionally cloaked against the cold,

He bowed as in a weary deference
To childish fate. "Surely I know you, Madam;
You are among the creatures of distinction
Whose quality may be seen even in the dark.
You are Queen Morgan, a most famous lady,
And one that only kings in holy joy
Could ask or dream to be their messenger.
What new persuasion has the King conceived
Beyond this inspiration of your presence?"

"It is not dark," she said; "or not so dark
But that a woman sees—if she be careful
Not to fall down these memorable stairs
And break her necessary little neck
At Tristram's feet. And you might make of that
Only another small familiar triumph
Hardly worth sighing for. Well then, the King
Is vexed and vicious. Your man Gouvernail
Says you are sick with wine. Was that the best
That your two heads together could accomplish?
Will you not for the King's sake, or the Queen's,
Be more compliant, and not freeze to death?"

"Madam, say to the King that if the King
Command me, I will come. Having said that,

It would be gracious of you to be merry—
Malicious, if you must—and say, also,
You found in me a melancholy warning
For all who dim their wits obliviously.
Say it as delicately or as directly
As humors your imperial preference."

Queen Morgan, coming closer, put a small
And cat-like hand on Tristram: "In this world
Of lies, you lay a burden on my virtue
When you would teach me a new alphabet.
I'll turn my poor wits inside out, of course,
Telling an angry king how sick you are—
With wine or whatsoever. Though I shall know
The one right reason why you are not merry,
I'll never scatter it, not for the King's life—
Though I might for the Queen's. Isolt should live,
If only to be sorry she came here—
With you—away from Ireland to be married
To a man old enough to bury himself.
But kings are kings, and by contriving find
Ways over many walls. This being their fate,
It was a clever forethought of the Lord

That there should be a woman or two left
With even Isolt no longer possible.
A school of prudence would establish you
Among the many whose hearts have bled and healed."

"Madam, you are a woman and a queen;
Wherefore a man, by force of courtesy,
Will hardly choose but listen. No doubt your words
Have a significance in their disguise;
Yet having none for me, they might be uttered
As well in a lost language found on ruins
As in our northern manner. If kings are kings
In your report, queens, I perceive, are queens,
And have their ways also."

       "A sort of queen."
She laughed, showing her teeth and shining eyes,
And shrugged herself a little nearer to him,
Having not far to come: "But not the sort
That makes a noise where now there are so many.
If silly men pursue me and make songs
About me, it may be because they've heard
Some legend that I'm strange. I am not strange—
Not half so strange as you are."

Tristram saw

Before him a white neck and a white bosom
Beneath a fair and feline face whereon
Demure determination was engraved
As on a piece of moonlit living marble,
And could at once have smiled and sighed to see
So much premeditated danger wasted
On his despair and wrath. "Yes, you are strange,"
He said, "and a sagacious peril to men—
Wherefore they must pursue you and make songs.
You are an altogether perilous lady,
And you had best go back now to the King,
Saying that I'm not well. I would conserve
The few shreds left of my integrity
From your displeasure and for wiser vision.
Say to the King I feasted over much
In recognition of his happiness—
An error that apology too soon
Might qualify too late. Tell the King so,
And I am your obedient slave for ever.

A wry twist, all but imperceptible
Disfigured for an instant her small mouth
[33]

Before she smiled and said: "We are the slaves,
Not you. Not even when most we are in power
Are women else than slaves to men they honor.
Men worthy of their reverence know this well,
And honor them sometimes to humor them.
We are their slaves and their impediments,
And there is much in us to be forgiven."

He drew the fringes of her cloak together,
Smiling as one who suffers to escape
Through silence to familiar misery.
"Madam, I fear that you are taking cold,"
He said. "Say to the King that I'm not well."
She laughed, and having mounted a few steps
Paused and looked down at him inscrutably:
"'An error that apology too soon
May qualify too late?' Was it like that?
England is not so large as the wide sky
That holds the stars, and we may meet again.
Good night, Sir Tristram, Prince of Lyonesse."

III

Lost in a gulf of time where time was lost,
And heedless of a light queen's light last words
That were to be remembered, he saw now

Before him in the gloom a ghostly ship
Cleaving a way to Cornwall silently
From Ireland, with himself on board and one
That with her eyes told him intolerably
How little of his blind self a crowded youth,
With a sight error-flecked and pleasure-flawed,
Had made him see till on that silent voyage
There was no more to see than faith betrayed
Or life disowned.   The sorrow in his name
Came out, and he was Tristram, born for sorrow
Of an unguarded and forgotten mother,
Who may have seen as those who are to die
Are like to see.   A king's son, he had given
Himself in honor unto another king
For gratitude, not knowing what he had given,
Or seeing what he had done.   Now he could see,
And there was no need left of a ship's ghost,
Or ghost of anything else than life before him,
To make him feel, though he might not yet hear it,
The nearness of a doom that was descending
Upon him, and anon should hold him fast—
If he were not already held fast enough
To please the will of fate.

                              "Brangwaine!" he said,
Turning and trembling. For a softer voice
Than Morgan's now had spoken; a truer voice,
Which had not come alone to plead with him
In the King's name for courtesy.

                                    "Sir Tristram! . . ."
Brangwaine began, and ended. Then she seized
His hands and held them quickly to her lips
In fealty that he felt was his for ever.
"Brangwaine, for this you make a friend of me
Until I die. If there were more for one
To say . . ." He said no more, for some one else
Than Brangwaine was above him on the stairs.
Coming down slowly and without a sound
She moved, and like a shadow saying nothing
Said nothing while she came. Isolt of Ireland,
With all her dark young majesty unshaken
By grief and shame and fear that made her shake
Till to go further would have been to fall,
Came nearer still to him and still said nothing,
Till terror born of passion became passion
Reborn of terror while his lips and hers
                        [36]

Put speech out like a flame put out by fire.
The music poured unheard, Brangwaine had vanished,
And there were these two in the world alone,
Under the cloudy light of a cold moon
That glimmered now as cold on Brittany
As on Cornwall.

Time was aware of them,
And would beat soon upon his empty bell
Release from such a fettered ecstasy
As fate would not endure.   But until then
There was no room for time between their souls
And bodies, or between their silences,
Which were for them no less than heaven and hell,
Fused cruelly out of older silences
That once a word from either might have ended,
And so annihilated into life
Instead of death—could her pride then have spoken,
And his duped eyes have seen, before his oath
Was given to make them see.   But silences
By time are slain, and death, or more than death,
May come when silence dies.   At last Isolt
Released herself enough to look at him,

With a world burning for him in her eyes,
And two worlds crumbling for him in her words:
"What have I done to you, Tristram!" she said;
"What have you done to me! What have we done
To Fate, that she should hate us and destroy us,
Waiting for us to speak. What have we done
So false or foul as to be burned alive
And then be buried alive—as we shall be—
As I shall be!"

   He gazed upon a face
Where all there was of beauty and of love
That was alive for him, and not for him,
Was his while it was there. "I shall have burned
And buried us both," he said. "Your pride would not
Have healed my blindness then, even had you prayed
For God to let you speak. When a man sues
The fairest of all women for her love,
He does not cleave the skull first of her kinsman
To mark himself a man. That was my way;
And it was not the wisest—if your eyes
Had any truth in them for a long time.
Your pride would not have let me tell them more—
Had you prayed God, I say."

"I did do that,
Tristram, but he was then too far from heaven
To hear so little a thing as I was, praying
For you on earth. You had not seen my eyes
Before you fought with Morhaus; and for that,
There was your side and ours. All history sings
Of two sides, and will do so till all men
Are quiet; and then there will be no men left,
Or women alive to hear them. It was long
Before I learned so little as that; and you
It was who taught me while I nursed and healed
Your wound, only to see you go away."

"And once having seen me go away from you,
You saw me coming back to you again,
Cheerful and healed, as Mark's ambassador.
Would God foresee such folly alive as that
In any thing he had made, and still make more?
If so, his ways are darker than divines
Have drawn them for our best bewilderments.
Be it so or not, my share in this is clear.
I have prepared a way for us to take,
Because a king was not so much a devil

When I was young as not to be a friend,
An uncle, and an easy counsellor.
Later, when love was yet no more for me
Than a gay folly glancing everywhere
For triumph easier sometimes than defeat,
Having made sure that I was blind enough,
He sealed me with an oath to make you his
Before I had my eyes, or my heart woke
From pleasure in a dream of other faces
That now are nothing else than silly skulls
Covered with skin and hair. The right was his
To make of me a shining knight at arms,
By fortune may be not the least adept
And emulous. But God! for seizing you,
And having you here tonight, and all his life
Having you here, by the blind means of me,
I could tear all the cords out of his neck
To make a rope, and hang the rest of him.
Isolt, forgive me! This is only sound
That I am making with a tongue gone mad
That you should be so near me as to hear me
Saying how far away you are to go
When you go back to him, driven by—me!

A fool may die with no great noise or loss;
And whether a fool should always live or not . . ."

Isolt, almost as with a frightened leap
Muffled his mouth with hers in a long kiss,
Blending in their catastrophe two fires
That made one fire. When she could look at him
Again, her tears, unwilling still to flow,
Made of her eyes two shining lakes of pain
With moonlight living in them; and she said
"There is no time for you to tell me this;
And you are younger than time says you are,
Or you would not be losing it, saying over
All that I know too well, or for my sake
Giving yourself these names that are worth nothing.
It was our curse that you were not to see
Until you saw too late. No scourge of names
That you may lay for me upon yourself
Will have more consequence for me, or you,
Than beating with a leaf would have on horses;
So give yourself no more of them tonight.
The King says you are coming back with me.
How can you come? And how can you not come!

[41]

It will be cruel enough for me without you,
But with you there alive in the same walls
I shall be hardly worthy of life tonight
If I stay there alive—although I shall,
For this may not be all. This thing has come
For us, and you are not to see the end
Through any such fog of honor and self-hate
As you may seek to throw around yourself
For being yourself. Had you been someone else,
You might have been one like your cousin Andred,
Who looks at me as if he were a snake
That has heard something. Had you been someone else,
You might have been like Modred, or like Mark.
God—you like Mark! You might have been a slave.
We cannot say what either of us had been
Had we been something else. All we can say
Is that this thing has come to us tonight.
You can do nothing more unless you kill him,
And that would be the end of you and me.
Time on our side, this may not be the end."

"I might have been a slave, by you unseen,"
He answered, "and you still Isolt of Ireland,

To me unknown.   That would have been for you
The better way.   But that was not the way."

"No it was not," she said, trying to smile;
And weary then for trying, held him closer.
"But I can feel the hands of time on me,
And they will soon be tearing me away.
Tristram, say to me once before I go,
What you believe and what you see for us
Before you.   Are you sure that a word given
Is always worth more than a world forsaken?
Who knows there may not be a lonely place
In heaven for souls that are ashamed and sorry
For fearing hell?"

                    "It is not hell tonight,
Isolt," he said, "or any beyond the grave,
That I fear most for you or for myself.
Fate has adjusted and made sure of that
Where we are now—though we see not the end,
And time be on our side.   Praise God for time,
And for such hope of what may come of it
As time like this may grant.   I could be strong,

But to be over-strong now at this hour
Would only be destruction. The King's ways
Are not those of one man against another,
And you must live, and I must live—for you.
If there were not an army of guards below us
To bring you back to fruitless ignominy,
There would soon be an end of this offense
To God and the long insult of this marriage.
But to be twice a fool is not the least
Insane of ways to cure a first affliction.
God!—is it so—that you are going back
To be up there with him—with Mark—tonight?
Before you came, I had been staring down
On those eternal rocks and the white foam
Around them; and I thought how sound and long
A sleep would soon begin for us down there
If we were there together—before you came.
That was a fancy, born of circumstance,
And I was only visioning some such thing
As that. The moon may have been part of it.
I think there was a demon born with me
And in the malediction of my name,
And that his work is to make others suffer—

Which is the worst of burdens for a man
Whose death tonight were nothing, could the death
Of one be the best end of this for two."

"If that was to be said," Isolt replied,
"It will at least not have to be said over.
For since the death of one would only give
The other a twofold weight of wretchedness
To bear, why do you pour these frozen words
On one who cannot be so confident
As you that we may not be nearer life,
Even here tonight, than we are near to death?
I must know more than you have told me yet
Before I see, so clearly as you see it,
The sword that must for ever be between us.
Something in you was always in my father.
A darkness always was around my father,
Since my first eyes remembered him. He saw
Nothing, but he would see the shadow of it
Before he saw the color or shape it had,
Or where the sun was. Tristram, fair things yet
Will have a shadow black as night before them,
And soon will have a shadow black as night

Behind them. And all this may be a shadow,
Sometime, that we may live to see behind us—
Wishing that we had not been all so sure
Tonight that it was always to be night."

"Your father may have fancied where the sun was
When first he saw the shadow of King Mark
Coming with mine before me. You are brave
Tonight, my love. A bravery like yours now
Would be the summons for a mightier love
Than mine, if there were room for such a love
Among things hidden in the hearts of men.
Isolt! Isolt! . . ."

                    Out of her struggling eyes
There were tears flowing, and withheld in his,
Tears were a veil of pity and desperation
Through which he saw the dim face of Isolt
Before him like a phantom in a mist—
Till to be sure that she was not a phantom,
He clutched and held her fast against his heart,
And through the cloak she wore felt the warm life
Within her trembling to the life in him,

And to the sorrow and the passion there
That would be always there. "Isolt! Isolt!"
Was all the language there was left in him
And she was all that was left anywhere—
She that would soon be so much worse than gone
That if he must have seen her lying still,
Dead where she was, he could have said that fate
Was merciful at least to one of them.
He would have worn through life a living crown
Of death, for memory more to be desired
Than any furtive and forsworn desire,
Or shattered oath of his to serve a King,
His mother's brother, without wilful stain,
Was like to be with all else it might be.
So Tristram, in so far as there was reason
Left in him, would have reasoned—when Isolt
Drew his face down to hers with all her strength,
Or so it seemed, and kissed his eyes and cheeks
And mouth until there was no reason left
In life but love—love that was not to be,
Save as a wrenching and a separation
Past reason or reprieve.   If she forgot
For long enough to smile at him through tears,

[47]

He may have read it as a sign that God
Was watching her and all might yet be well:
And if he knew that all might not be well,
Some God might still be watching over her,
With no more power than theirs now against Rome,
Or the pernicious valor of sure ruin,
Or against fate, that like an unseen ogre
Made hungry sport of these two there alone
Above the moaning wash of Cornish water,
Cold upon Cornish rocks.

                              "No bravery, love,"
She said, "or surely none like mine, would hide,
Among things in my heart that are not hidden,
A love larger than all time and all places,
And stronger beyond knowledge than all numbers
Around us that can only make us dead
When they are done with us.   Tristram, believe
That if I die my love will not be dead,
As I believe that yours will not be dead.
If in some after time your will may be
To slay it for the sake of a new face,
It will not die.   Whatever you do to it.

It will not die. We cannot make it die,
We are not mighty enough to sentence love
Stronger than death to die, though we may die.
I do not think there is much love like ours
Here in this life, or that too much of it
Would make poor men and women who go alone
Into their graves without it more content,
Or more by common sorrow to be envied
Than they are now. This may be true, or not.
Perhaps I am not old enough to know —
Not having lived always, nor having seen
Much else than everything disorderly
Deformed to order into a small court,
Where love was most a lie. Might not the world,
If we could sift it into a small picture,
Be more like that than it would be like—this?
No, there is not much like this in the world—
And there may not be this!"

                              Tristram could see
Deep in the dark wet splendor of her eyes,
A terror that he knew was more for him
Than for herself. "You are still brave enough,"

He said, "and you might look to me for strength.
If I were a magician and a wizard,
To vanquish the invincible.   Destruction
Of such a sort as one here among hundreds
Might wreak upon himself would be a pastime,
If ruin of him would make you free again
Without him."

                    "I would not be free without him,"
Isolt said, as if angry: "And you know
That I should not be free if I were free
Without him.   Say no more about destruction
Till we see more, who are not yet destroyed.
O God, if only one of us had spoken—
When there was all that time!"

                    "You mean by that,
If only I had spoken," Tristram said;
And he could say no more till her quick lips
That clung to his again would let him speak.
"You mean, if only I had been awake
In paradise, instead of asleep there,
No jealous angel with a burning sword
[50]

Would have had power enough to drive me out,
Though God himself had sent him."

                                        Isolt smiled,
As with a willing pity, and closed her eyes
To keep more tears from coming out of them;
And for a time nothing was to be heard
Except the pounding of two hearts in prison,
The torture of a doom-begotten music
Above them, and the wash of a cold foam
Below them on those cold eternal rocks
Where Tristram and Isolt had yesterday
Come to be wrecked together.   When her eyes
Opened again, he saw there, watching him,
An aching light of memory; and his heart
Beat harder for remembering the same light
That he had seen before in the same eyes.

"Alone once in the moonlight on that ship,"
She said, still watching him and clinging warm
Against him, "I believed that you would speak,
For I could hear your silence like a song
Out of the sea.   I stood by the ship's rail,

Looking away into the night, with only
You and the ocean and the moon and stars
There with me.   I was not seeing where I looked,
For I had waited too long for your step
Behind me to care then if the ship sailed
Or sank, so long as one true word of yours
Went wheresoever the ship went with me.
If these eyes, that were looking off so far
Over the foam, found anything there that night
Worth looking at, they have forgotten it;
And if my ears heard even the waves that night,
Or if my cheeks felt even the wind that night,
They have forgotten waves and wind together,
Remembering only there was you somewhere
On the same ship where I was, all alone
As I was, and alive   When you did come,
At last, and were there with me, and still silent,
You had already made yourself in vain
The loyal counterfeit of someone else
That never was, and I hope never shall be,
To make me sure there was no love for me
To find in you, where love was all I found.
You had not quite the will or quite the wish,

Knowing King Mark, not to reveal yourself,
When revelation was no more the need
Of my far larger need than revelation.
There was enough revealed, but nothing told.
Since I dare say to you how sure I am
Of the one thing that's left me to be sure of,
Know me and love me as I was that night,
As I am now, and as I shall be always—
All yours; and all this means for you and me
Is no small care for you. If you had spoken
There on that ship what most was in your heart
To say—if you had held me close—like this—
If you had kissed me then—like this—I wonder
If there would have been kings and crowns enough
In Cornwall or in England or elsewhere
To make the crowns of all kings everywhere
Shine with a light that would have let me see
No king but you and no crown but our love.
Tristram, believe, whatever the rest may be,
This is all yours—for God to weigh at last,
And as he will. And if it be found wanting,
He will not find what's left so ordinary
As not to say of it, 'This was Isolt—

Isolt who was all love.' He made her so,
And some time he may tell her why it is
So many that are on earth are there to suffer.
I say this now, for time will not wait always,
And we shall not be here when we are old—
If time can see us old.   I had not thought
Of that; and will not think of it again.
There must be women who are made for love,
And of it, and are mostly pride and fire
Without it.   There would not be much else left
Of them without it than sold animals
That might as well be driven and eating grass
As weaving, riding, hunting, and being queens,
Or not being queens.   But when two loves like ours
Wear down the wall of time dividing them,
Two oceans come together and flow over
Time and his evil work.   It was too long,
That wall, but there is nothing left of it,
And there is only love where the wall was.
And while you love me you will not forget
That you are all there is in my life now
That I would live for longer.   And since nothing
Is left to me but to be sure of nothing

That you have not been sure of and been told,
You can believe me, though you cannot save me.
No, there is only one way to do that. . . .
If I were sure this was to be the end,
I should make this the end . . . Tristram! Tristram!
With you in the same house!"

                                  "Do not say that."
He shook, and held her face away from him,
Gazing upon it as a man condemned
To darkness might have gazed for the last time
At all there was of life that he should see
Before his eyes were blinded by white irons.
"Tell me to throw myself over this wall,
Down upon those dead rocks, and I will do it.
Tell me to fall down now upon the point
Of this too restive sword, and you will see
How brief a sting death has. Tell me to drink
Tonight the most efficient mortal poison,
And of all drink that may be poured tomorrow
None shall be poured for me. But do not say,
Or make me say, where I shall be tonight.
All I can say is, I shall not be here.

Something within me is too near to breaking,
And it is not my heart. That will not break,
Nor shall a madness that is in me now
Break time in two—time that is on our side.
Yet I would see as little of Mark tonight
As may be well for my forgetfulness.
That was the best for me to say to you,
For now it has been said, I shall not kill him."

She trembled in his arms, and with a cry
Of stricken love gave all there was of her
That she could give to him in one more kiss
In which the world was melted and was nothing
For them but love—until another cry,
From Brangwaine, all forgotten in the garden,
Made the world firm again. He leapt away,
Leaving Isolt bewildered and heart-sick
With fear for him, and for she knew not what,
And lastly for herself. But soon she felt
A noise that was like one of shadows fighting.
Then she saw Tristram, who was bringing with him
A choking load that he dragged after him;
And then she could see Brangwaine, white as death

Behind those two. And while she saw them there,
She could hear music from those walls above her,
And waves foaming on the cold rocks below.

When Tristram spoke, his words came hoarse and few.
"I knew the vermin I should find," he said,
And said no more. He muttered and hurled something
Away from him against the parapet,
Hearing the sound that a skull makes on stone;
And without looking one way or another,
He stood there for a time like a man struck
By doom to an ungovernable silence,
Breathing above the crumpled shape of Andred.

IV

Tristram, like one bereft of all attention,
Saw little and heard nothing until Isolt
Sprang with a gasp and held her lips to his
An instant, and looked once into his eyes
Before she whispered in his ears a name,
And sprang away from him. But this was not
Before King Mark had seen sufficiently
To find himself a shadow and Tristram

The substance of it in his Queen's cold eyes,
Which were as dark and dead to him as death
And had no answers in them.

                    "Gouvernail,"
The King said, after staring angrily
About him, "who is lying there at your feet?
Turn him, and let me see?"

                    "You know him, sir,"
Tristram replied, in tones of no address:
"The name of that you see down there is Andred;
And it is manifestly at your service."

"That was an unbecoming jest, I fear,
For you tonight, Tristram," answered the King.
"Do you not see what you have done to him?
Andred is bleeding."

                    "I am glad of that, sir.
So long as there is less of that bad blood
In him, there will be so much less of Andred.
Wash him, and he will be as good as ever;

[58]

And that will be about as good as warts.
If I had been abrupt with him and drowned him,
I'd pity the sick fishes." Tristram's words,
Coming he knew not whence, fell without life
As from a tongue without it.

                    "Gouvernail,"
The King said, trembling in his desperation,
"The Queen and Brangwaine will go back with you.
Come down again with two men of the guard,
And when you come, take Andred through the garden."

"And through the little window he came out of,"
Said Tristram, in the way of one asleep.
Then, seeing the King as if for the first time,
He turned his head to see Isolt once more,
Vanishing, and to see for many a night
And day the last look in her frightened eyes.
But not inured yet fully to his doom,
He waited for the King to speak.

                    "Tristram,"
He said, in words wherein his pride and fury
Together achieved almost an incoherence,

"My first right is to ask what Andred saw
That you should so mistreat him. Do not hide
Yourself in silence, for I saw enough."

Tristram's initial answer was a shrug
Of reckless hate before he spoke: "Well, sir,
If you have seen enough, what matters it
How little or much this thing here may have seen?
His reptile observation must have gathered
Far less than you prepared him to report.
There was not much to see that I remember."

"There was no preparation on my part,
And Andred's act was of a loyalty
As well intentioned as it was unsought
And unforeseen by me. I swear to this,
Tristram. Is there as much of truth in you
As that, or is there nothing you dare name
Left of you now that may survive an oath?"

"I know these kings' beginnings," Tristram said,
Too furious to be prudent, "and I know
The crafty clutch of their advantages

[60]

Over the small who cringe.   And it appears
That a place waits for my apology
To fill for one thing left to thank God for."

"Tomorrow, if occasion shows itself,
Tristram, you may thank God you are alive.
Your plea for pardon has the taint of doubt
Upon it; yet I shall make a minute of it,
Here by the smudge of a sick lamp that smells
Of all I thought was honor."

                    Tristram saw
Confronting him two red and rheumy eyes,
Pouched in a face that nature had made comely,
And in appearance was indulgently
Ordained to wait on lust and wine and riot
For more years yet than leeches might foresee.
Meeting the crafty sadness always in them,
He found it more than sad and worse than crafty,
And saw that no commingled shame and rage
Like that which he could see in them tonight
Would go out soon.   "Damn such a man," he thought
And inward pain made sweat upon his forehead.
"I could almost believe that he believed

Himself, if I had never known him better.
Possession has a blade that will go deep
Unless I break it; and if I do that,
I shall break with it everything. Isolt!
Isolt and honor are the swords he'll use,
Leaving me mine that I've sworn not to use.
Honor—from him? If he found Honor walking
Here in Cornwall, he would send men to name it,
And would arrest it as a trespasser.
How does one take a thrust that pierces two,
And still defend the other from destruction?''

"Well, Tristram, knight-at-arms and man of honor,"
Mark said, "what last assay have you for me
Of honor now? If you were not the son
Of my dead sister, I should be oppressed
To say how long the sight of you alive
Would be the living cross that my forbearance
Might have to bear. But no, not quite that, either.
I can at least expunge the sight of you
Henceforth from Cornwall, if you care to live.''

"Nowhere among my fancies here tonight, sir,
Is there a wish to live and be a cross

Upon your shoulders. If you find a figure
More salient and germane to my condition,
I might then care to live. Your point of honor,
Reduced obscurely to a nothingness,
Would hardly be a solid resting-place,
Or a safe one, for me. Give me the choice
Of death, or of inflicting more than death,
I would not live from now until tomorrow.
All said, what have I done? What you have seen.
And if there's any man or Andred breathing
Who tells you lies of more than you have seen,
Give me his name, and he'll tell no more lies.
Andred is waking up; and if I've ears,
Here are those guards coming with Gouvernail.
Andred, if you were not my lizard-cousin,
You might not be awake."

                       "I heard that, Tristram,"
Groaned a low voice. "I shall remember that.
I heard the Queen say, 'Tristram, I'm all yours—
All yours!' And then she kissed you till her mouth
Might have been part of yours. 'All yours! All yours!'
Let the King say if I'm a lizard now,

Or if I serve him well."   He snarled and spat
At Tristram, who, forgetting, drew his sword,
And after staring at it in the moonlight
Replaced it slowly and reluctantly.

"I cannot kill a worm like that," he said.
Yet a voice tells me I had better do so.
Take him away—or let the King say that.
This is no slave of mine."

                              Gouvernail's men
Stood as if waiting for the moon to fall
Into the sea, but the King only nodded,
Like one bemused; and Andred, with an arm
Thrown over each of them, stumbled away.
The King gave one more nod, and Gouvernail,
Like sorrow in the mould of a bowed man,
Went slowly after him.

                              Then the King said,
"Tristram, I cannot trust myself much longer,
With you before me, to be more than man."
His fury shook him into a long silence
[64]

That had an end in tears of helpless rage:
"Why have you come between me and my Queen,
Stealing her love as you might steal my gold!
Honor! Good God in heaven! Is this honor—
And after all that I have done for you?"

"Almost as much as buying her with gold,
Or its equivalent in peace, was honor.
And as for all that you have done for me,
There are some tenuous items on my side.
Did I not, fighting Morhaus in your name,
Rid Cornwall of a tribute that for years
Had sucked away the blood and life of Cornwall,
Like vampires feeding on it in the night?
And have I not in my blind gratitude
For kindness that would never have been yours
If it had cost you even a night's rest,
Brought you for Queen the fairest of all women?
If these two gifts, which are but two, were all,
What more, in the King's name, would the King ask?"

"The casuistries of youth will not go far
With me, Tristram. You brought to me a Queen,

Stealing her love while you were bringing her.
What weakness is it in me lets you live?"

"I beg your pardon, sir, and for one error.
Where there was never any love to steal,
No love was ever stolen. Honor—oh, yes!
If all the rituals, lies, and jigs and drinking
That make a marriage of an immolation—"

"By heaven, if you say one more word like that,"
The King cried, with his sword half out again,
"One of us will be left here!" Then he stopped,
As if a bat had flown against his ear
And whispered of the night. "But I will cease,
Mindful of who you are, with one more question.
You cast a cloud around the name of honor
As if the sight of it were none too sweet
In your remembrance. If it be not honor
That ails you now and makes a madman of you,
It may be there's a reptile with green eyes
Arrived for a long feeding on your heart—
Biting a bit, who knows?"

                                Tristram could see
In the King's eyes the light of a lewd smile

That angrily deformed his aging face
With an avenging triumph. "Is this your **way**
To make a madman of me? If it be so,
Before you take my reason, take my life.
But no—you cannot. You have taken that."
He drew his sword as if each gleaming inch
Had come in anguish out of his own flesh,
And would have given it for the King to keep—
Fearing himself, in his malevolence,
Longer to be its keeper. But the King,
Seizing his moment, gave Tristram no time
More than to show the trembling steel, and hear
The doom that he had felt and partly seen
With Isolt's hope to cheer him.

                        "You have drawn
Your sword against the King, Tristram," he said.
"Now put it back. Your speech to me before
Was nearer your last than you are near to me—
Yet I'll not have your blood. I'll have your life,
Instead—since you are sure your life means only
One woman—and will keep it far from you;
So far that you shall hunger for it always.

When you go down those stairs for the last time,
And that time will be now, you leave Cornwall
Farther behind you than hell's way from heaven
Is told in leagues. And if the sight of you
Offends again my kingdom and infects it,
I swear by God you will be chained and burned.
And while you burn, her eyes will be held open
To watch your passion cooling in the flames.
Go!—and may all infernal fires attend you—
You and your nights and days, and all your dreams
Of her that you have not, and shall have never!"

"You know that for her sake, and for that only,
You are alive to say this," Tristram said;
And after one look upward at those lights
That soon would all be out, he swayed and trembled,
And slowly disappeared down the long stairs,
Passing the guards who knew him with a word
Of empty cheer, regardless of what thoughts
Of theirs were following him and his departure,
Which had no goal but the pursuing clutch
Of a mad retrospect.

                              He strode along
Until there was no moon but a white blur

Low in a blurred gray sky, and all those lights
That once had shone above him and Isolt,
And all that clamor of infernal joy
That once had shrilled above him and Isolt,
Were somewhere miles away among the ages
That he had walked and counted with his feet,
Which he believed, or dreamed that he believed,
Were taking him through hell to Camelot.
There he would send, or so again he dreamed,
A word to Lancelot or to Gawaine,
But what word he knew not.   There was no word,
Save one, that he could seize and separate
Out of the burning fury and regret
That made a fire of all there was of him
That he could call himself.   And when slow rain
Fell cold upon him as upon hot fuel,
It might as well have been a rain of oil
On faggots round some creature at a stake.
For all the quenching there was in it then
Of a sick sweeping heat consuming him
With anguish of intolerable loss,
Which might be borne if it were only loss.
But there was with it, always and again,

[69]

A flame-lit picture of Isolt alone
With Mark, in his embrace, and with that mouth
Of his on hers, and that white body of hers
Unspeakably imprisoned in his arms
For nights and days and years.   A time had been
When by the quick destruction of all else
And of himself, he might have spared Isolt
By leaving her alone for lonely pain
To prey on till she died and followed him
To whatsoever the dusk-hidden doors
Of death might hide for such a love as theirs;
And there was nothing there so foul, he thought—
So far as he could think—and out of reason,
As to be meted for a sin like theirs
That was not sin, but fate—which must itself
Be but a monstrous and unholy jest
Of sin stronger than fate, sin that had made
The world for love—so that the stars in heaven
Might laugh at it, and the moon hide from it,
And the rain fall on it, and a King's guile
And lust makes one more shuddering toy of it.
He would not see behind him, yet had eyes
That saw behind him and saw nowhere else.

Before him there was nothing left to see
But lines of rain that he could hardly see,
And shapes that had no shape along a road
That had no sodden end. So on he strode
Without a guiding end in sight or mind,
Save one, if there were such an end somewhere,
That suddenly might lead him off the world
To sink again into the mysteries
From which his love had come, to which his love
Would drag him back again with ropes of fire
Behind him in the rain at which he laughed,
As in his torture he might then have laughed
At heaven from hell. He had seen both tonight—
Two had seen both, and two for one were chosen,
Because a love that was to be fulfilled
Only in death, was for some crumbs of hope,
Which he had shared for mercy with Isolt,
Foredoomed to live—how or how long to live
With him, he knew not. If it lived with him
Tonight, it lived only as things asleep
In the same rain where he was not asleep
Were somewhere living, as tomorrow's light
Would prove they were. Tomorrow's light, he thought,

Might prove also that he was living once,
And that Isolt was living once where lamps
Were shining and where music dinned and shrieked
Above her, and cold waves foaming on rocks
Below her called and hushed and called again
To say where there was peace.

                                    There was no peace
For Tristram until after two nights' walking,
And two days' ranging under dripping trees,
No care was left in him to range or walk,
Or to be found alive where finally,
Under an aged oak he cast himself,
Falling and lying as a man half dead
Might shape himself to die. Before he slept,
A shame came over him that he, Tristram,
A man stronger than men stronger than he,
Should now be weaker than a man unmade
By slow infirmity into a child
To be the sport of children. Then his rage
Put shame away and was again a madness,
And then a blank, wherein not even a name
That he remembered would stay long enough

For him to grasp it or to recognize it,
Before the ghost of what had been a name
Would vanish like a moonbeam on a tomb
When a cloud comes. Cloud after cloud came fast,
Obliterating before leaving clear
The word that he had lost. It was a name
Of some one far behind him in the gloom,
Where there were lights above, and music sounding,
And the long wash of a cold sea below.
"Isolt!" He smiled as one who from a dream
Wakes to find he was dreaming and not dying,
And then he slept.

When he awoke again,
It was to find around him, after fever,
A squalid box of woodland poverty
In which he lay like a decrepit worm
Within an empty shell. Through a small square
Clear sunlight slanted, and there was outside
A scattered sound of life that fitfully
Twittered and shrilled. In time there was a tread
Of heavy steps, and soon a door was open;
Then in from somewhere silently there came

[73]

A yokel shape, unsightly and half-clad,
That shambled curiously but not unkindly
Towards the low sodden pallet where Tristram
Lay wondering where he was; and after him
Came one that he remembered with a leap
Of gladness in his heart.

                    "You—Gouvernail?"
He cried; and he fell back into a swoon
Of uselessness too deep for Gouvernail
To call him from by kindly word or touch
Till time was ready.   In the afternoon,
Tristram, not asking what had come to pass,
Nor caring much, found himself in a cart,
Dimly aware of motion and low words
And of a dull security.   He slept,
And half awoke, and slept again, till stones
Under the wheels and a familiar glimpse
Of unfamiliar walls around a court
Told of a journey done.   That night he slept,
And in the morning woke to find himself
In a place strange to him.   Whose place it was,
Or why he should be in it, was no matter.

There he could rest, and for a time forget.
So, for a time, he lost the name of life,
And of all else except Isolt. . . . "Isolt!"
That was the only name left in the world,
And that was only a name.   "Isolt! Isolt!"

After an endless day of sleep and waking,
With Gouvernail adventuring in and out
Like some industrious and unquiet phantom,
He woke again with low light coming in
Through a red window. Now the room was dim,
But with a dimness that would let him see
That he was not alone.   "Isolt!" he said,
And waited, knowing that it was not Isolt.

A crooning voice that had within its guile
A laughing ring of metal said, "Isolt?
Isolt is married. Are you young men never
To know that when a princess weds a king
The young man, if he be a wise young man,
Will never afford himself another fever,
And lie for days on a poor zany's rags,
For all the princesses in Christendom?
Gouvernail found you, I found Gouvernail,

And here you are, my lord. Forget Isolt,
And care a little for your royal self;
For you may be a king one of these days
And make some other young man as miserable
As Mark makes you. The world appears to be,
Though God knows why, just such a place as that.
Remember you are safe, and say your prayers.
For all you know of this life or the next,
You may be safer here than in your shroud.
Good night, Sir Tristram, Prince of Lyonesse."

Days after, vexed with doubt and indecision,
Queen Morgan, with her knight a captive now,
Sat gazing at him in a coming twilight,
Partly in anger, partly in weary triumph,
And more than all in a dark wonderment
Of what enchantment there was wanting in her
To keep this man so long out of her toll
Of willing remnants and of eager cinders,
Now scattered and forgotten save as names
To make her smile. If she sat smiling now,
It was not yet for contemplated havoc
Of this man's loyalty to a lost dream

Where she was nothing. She had made other men
Dream themselves dead for her, but not this man,
Who sat now glowering with a captive scorn
Before her, waiting grimly for a word
Of weariness or of anger or disdain
To set him free.

                    "You are not sound enough,
My lord, for travel yet," she said. "I know,
For I have done more delving into life
And death than you, and into this mid-region
Between them, where you are, and where you sit
So cursed with loneliness and lethargy
That I could weep. Hard as this is for you,
It might be worse. You will go on your way,
While I sit knitting, withering and outworn,
With never a man that looks at me, save you,
So truthful as to tell me so." She laughed
At him again, and he heard metal laughing,
As he had heard it speaking, in her low
And stinging words.

                    "You are not withering yet."
He said; and his eyes ranged forgetfully
Over a studied feline slenderness

Where frugal silk was not frugality.
"I am too ill to see, in your account,
More than how safe I am with you." Isolt,
With her scared violet eyes and blue-black hair
Flew like a spirit driven from a star
Into that room and for a moment stayed
Before him. In his eyes he could feel tears
Of passion, desperation, and remorse,
Compounded with abysmal indignation
At a crude sullen hunger not deceived,
Born of a sloth enforced and of a scorn
Transformed malignly to a slow surrender.
His captor, when she saw them, came to him
And with a mocking croon of mother-comfort
Fondled him like a snake with two warm arms
And a warm mouth; and after long chagrin
Of long imprisonment, and long prisoned hate
For her that in his hatred of himself
He sought now like an animal, he made
No more acknowledgment of her cajoling
Than suddenly to rise without a word
And carry her off laughing in his arms,
Himself in hers half strangled.

As heretofore, found waiting him again
The same cold uncommunicating guards,
Past whom there was no word.   Another day,
And still another and another day
Found them as mute in their obedience
As things made there of wood.   Tristram, within
Meanwhile achieved a sorry composition
Of loyalty and circumstance.   "Tomorrow,"
He said, "I must be out and on my way."
And Morgan only said, "Which way is that?"
And so on for a fortnight, when at last,
With anger in her eyes and injuries
Of his indifference envenoming
The venom in her passion and her pride,
She let him go—though not without a laugh
That followed him like steel piercing unseen
His flight away from her with Gouvernail.

"You leave me now," she said, "but Fate has eyes.
You are the only blind one who is here,
As you are still to see.   I said before,
Britain is less than the whole firmament,

And we may meet again.   Until we meet,
Farewell; and find somewhere a good physician
To draw the poison of a lost Isolt
Out of your sick young heart.   Till he do so,
You may as well be rearing you a tomb
That else will hold you—presently.   Farewell,
Farewell, Sir Tristram, Prince of Lyonesse,
The once redoubtable and undeceived,
Who now in his defeat would put Fate's eyes out.
Not yet, Sir Prince; and we may meet again."
She smiled; and a smile followed him long after
A sharp laugh was forgotten.

              Gouvernail,
Riding along with Tristram silently
Till there was no glimpse left of Morgan's prison
Through the still trees behind them, sighed and said
"Where are we going, Tristram, and what next?"
And through the kindness of his weary grief
There glimmered in his eyes a loyal smile
Unseen by Tristram, though as well divined
As if revealed.

        "You are the last of men,
And so the last of friends now, Gouvernail,

For me to cleave to in extremities
Beyond the malefactions of this world.
You are apart and indispensable,
Holding me out of madness until doom,
Which I feel waiting now like death in the dark,
Shall follow me and strike, unrecognized,
For the last time. Away from that snake's nest
Behind me, it would be enough to know
It is behind me, were it not for knowledge
That in a serpent that is unsubdued
And spurned, a special venom will be waiting
Its time. And when the serpent is a woman,
Or a thin brained and thinner blooded Andred,
Infirm from birth with a malignant envy,
One may not with one thrust annihilate
The slow disease of evil eating in them
For one that never willed them any evil.
Twice have I heard in helpless recognition
A voice to bid me strike. I have not struck,
And shall not . . . For a time now, Gouvernail,
My memory sees a land where there is peace,
And a good King whose world is in his kingdom
And in his quaint possession of a child

[81]

Whose innocence may teach me to be wise
Till I be strong again. I see a face
That once was fond of me, and a white hand
Holding an agate that I left in it.
I see a friendliness of old assured
In Brittany. If anywhere there were peace
For me, it might be there—or for some time
Till I'm awake and am a man again."

"I was not saying all that to you, Tristram,"
Gouvernail answered, looking at his reins,
"But since you say it, I'll not fatigue my tongue
Gainsaying it for no good. Time is a casket
Wherein our days are covered certainties
That we lift out of it, one after one,
For what the day may tell. Your day of doom,
Tristram, may like as not be one for you
To smile at, could you see it where it waits,
Far down, I trust, with many a day between
That shall have gladness in it, and more light
Than this day has. When you are on the sea,
And there are white waves everywhere to catch
The sunlight and dance with it and be glad

The sea was made, you may be glad also.
Youth sees too far to see how near it is
To seeing farther. You are too blind today,
By dim necessity of circumstance,
More than to guess. Whether you take your crown
In Lyonesse or not, you will be king
Wherever you are. Many by chance are crowned
As kings that are born rather to be tinkers,
Or farmers, or philosophers, or farriers,
Or barbers, or almost anything under God
Than to be kings. Whether you will or not,
You are a king, Tristram, for you are one
Of the time-sifted few that leave the world,
When they are gone, not the same place it was.
Mark what you leave."

                    "There was a good man once,",
Said Tristram, "who fed sunshine to the blind
Until the blind went mad, and the good man
Died of his goodness, and died violently.
If untoward pleasantries are your affection,
Say this was in your casket and not mine.
There's a contentious kingdom in myself

For me to rule before I shall rule others.
If it is not too dark for me to fight
In there for my advantage and advancement,
And if my armor holds itself together
So long as not to be disintegrated
Before it breaks and I am broken with it,
There may be such a king as you foresee;
And failing him, I shall not fail my friend,
Who shall not be forgotten.   Gouvernail,
Be glad that you have no more darkness in you."

They rode along in silence, Gouvernail
Retasting an abridgement undeserved,
And undeserving of another venture,
Or so his unofficial ardor warned him,
Into a darkness and a namelessness
Wherein his worldly and well-meaning eyes
Had never sought a name for the unseen.

V

Griffon, the giant scourge of Brittany,
Threatened while Tristram was appraising it,
In his anticipation, all the peace

Awaiting him across the foaming waves
That were to wash, in Gouvernail's invention,
Time out of life. And there King Howel's child,
Isolt of the white hands, living on hope,
Which in all seeming had itself alone
To live on, was for love and safety now
A prisoner in that castle by the sea
Where Tristram once, not thinking twice of it,
Had said that he would some day come again.
And more as a gay plaything than a pledge
Had left with her an agate which had been
For long her father's jest. It was her heart,
Which she had taken out of her white bosom,
He said, and in the forest or in the sea
Would presently be lost and never found
Again—not even for Tristram when he came.
But when he came there was no time for talk
Of hearts and agates. Welcome and wonderment
Appeased, and the still whiteness of Isolt
Regarded once and then at once forgotten,
Tristram, like one athirst with wine before him,
Heard the King's talk of a marauding host
That neither force nor craft had yet subdued

Or more than scattered, like an obscene flock
Of rooks alert around a living quarry
That might not have a longer while to live
Than a few days would hold, or not so many.

"Praise be to God, I could almost have said
For your ill fortune, sir, and for your danger,"
Was Tristram's answer to the King's grim news.
"I have been groping slowly out of life
Into a slough of darkness and disuse—
A place too far from either for life or death
To share with me.   Yes, I have had too much
Of what a fool, not knowing its right name,
Would call the joy of life.   If that be joy,
Give me a draught out of your cup of trouble,
And let it be seen then what's left of me
To deal with your bad neighbor.   For tonight,
Let me have rest before tomorrow's work,
Which may be early."

                    "Early and late, I fear,"
The King said, and eyed Tristram cautiously,
And with a melancholy questioning

Of much that was for him no more a question.
"If it be God that brings you here today,
I praise him in my thanks given to you,
Tristram, for this. Sleep, and forget tomorrow
Until tomorrow calls you. If ill comes
To you for this, I shall not wish to live—
But for my child. And if ill comes to her,
It will be death to live."

                              "Tomorrow, sir,
These ills may be the dregs in empty cups
With all the bitterness drunk out of them.
No ill shall come to her till you and I
And all your men go down defending her;
And I can figure no such havoc as that.
I'm not a thousand men, or more than one,
Yet a new mind and eye, and a new arm
At work with yours, may not combine for ruin."[28]

Uncertain afterwards in a foreseen
Achievement unachieved, Tristram rejoiced
At last when he saw Griffon at his feet
And saw the last of his pernicious minions

Dispatched or disappearing. And that night,
Having espied Isolt's forgotten harp,
He plucked and sang the shadow of himself,
To her his only self, unwittingly
Into the soul and fabric of her life,
Till death should find it there. So day by day
He fostered in his heart a tenderness
Unrecognized for more than a kind fear
For what imaginable small white pawn
Her candor and her flame-white loveliness
Could yet become for the cold game of kings,
Who might not always, if they would, play quite
Their game as others do.

                    Once by the shore
They lingered while a summer sun went down
Beyond the shining sea; and it was then
That sorrow's witchcraft, long at work in him,
Made pity out of sorrow, and of pity
Made the pale wine of love that is not love,
Yet steals from love a name. And while he felt
Within her candor and her artlessness
The still white fire of her necessity,

He asked in vain if this were the same fate
That for so long had played with him so darkly—
With him and with Isolt, Isolt of Ireland,
Isolt of the wild frightened violet eyes
That once had given him that last look of hers
Above the moaning call of those cold waves
On those cold Cornish rocks. This new Isolt,
This new and white Isolt, was nothing real
To him until he found her in his arms,
And, scarcely knowing how he found her there,
Kissed her and felt the sting of happy tears
On his bewildered lips. Her whiteness burned
Against him till he trembled with regret;
For hope so long unrealized real at last
To her, was perilously real to him.
He knew that while his life was in Cornwall,
Something of this white fire and loneliness
In Brittany must be his whereon to lavish
The comfort of kind lies while he should live.
There were some words that he would have been saying
When her eyes told him with a still reproof
That silence would say more; and Tristram wished
That silence might say all.

                    For a long time
They sat there, looking off across the water
Between them and Tintagel to the north,
Where Tristram saw himself chained to a stake
With flames around him and Isolt of Ireland
Held horribly to see. King Mark, he knew,
Would in his carnal rage cling to his word
And feast his eyes and hate insatiably
On his fulfilment of it—in itself
The least of Tristram's fear. It was her eyes,
Held open to behold him, that he saw,
More than it was himself, or any torture
That would be only torture worse than his
For her. He turned himself away from that,
And saw beside him two gray silent eyes
Searching in his with quaint solemnity
For some unspoken answer to a thought
Unspoken.

              "When I told my father first
That you would come, he only smiled at me,"
She said. "But I believe by saying always
That you were coming, he believed you would,
Just as I knew you would."

                       "And why was that.
My child?" he asked, a captive once again
To her gray eyes and her white need of him.
"You might have told your father I was coming
Till the world's end, and I might not have come."

"You would have come, because I knew you would,"
She said, with a smile shaking on her lips
And fading in her eyes. "And you said that,
Because you knew, or because you knew nothing,
Or cared less than you know. Because you knew,
I like to fancy. It will do no harm."

"Were I so sure of that," he thought, "as you are,
There would be no infection of regret
In my remembrance of a usefulness
That Brittany will say was mine. Isolt
Of Brittany? Why were two names like that
Written for me by fate upon my heart
In red and white? Is this white fire of pity,
If pity it be, to burn deeper than love?"
Isolt of Ireland's dark wild eyes before him
In the moonlight, and that last look of hers,
Appeared in answer. Tristram gazed away

Into the north, and having seen enough,
He turned again to find the same gray light
In the same eyes that searched in his before
For an unspoken answer to a thought
Unspoken. They came silently away,
And Tristram sang again to her that night.

And he sang many a time to her thereafter
Songs of old warriors, and old songs of love
Triumphant over wars that were forgotten;
And many a time he found in her gray eyes,
And in the rose-white warmth of her attention.
Dominion of a sure necessity
Beyond experience and the need of reason,
Which had at first amused him and at last
Had made him wonder why there should be tears
In a man's eyes for such a mild white thing
That had so quaint a wisdom in its mildness.
Unless because he watched it going slowly
Its mild white way out of the world without him.
"Can she see farther into time, by chance,
Than I do?" he would ask, observing her:
"She might do so, and still see little farther

Than to the patient ends of her white fingers
That are so much alive, like all of her."
She found him smiling, but in her large eyes
There was no smile. There was a need of him
That made him cold, as if a ghost had risen
Before him with a wordless admonition
That he must go or stay. And many a time
He would have gone, if he had not perforce
As many a time remained to sing for her
Those old songs over, and as many a time
Found in her gaze that sure necessity
Which held him with a wisdom beyond thought,
Or with an innocence beyond all wisdom,
Until he sang one night for the last time
To the King's child. For she was his child now,
And for as long as there was life in him
Was his to cherish and to wonder at,
That he should have this white wise fiery thing
To call his wife.

              "Magicians might have done it"
He pondered once, alone, "but in so far
As I'm aware of them, there are none left
In Brittany so adept as to achieve it.

Stars may have done it." Then King Howel, pleased,
Though in his pleasure as incredulous
As if he were somehow a little injured,
Appearing out of silence from behind him,
Took Tristram's hands approvingly in his,
And said, "You have a child that was a woma·
Before she was a child, and is today
Woman and child, and something not of either,
For you to keep or crush—without a sound
Of pain from her to tell you so. Beware
Somewhat of that, Tristram; and may you both
Be wise enough not to ask more of life
Than to be life, and fate." The last word fell
Like a last coin released unwillingly
By caution giving all. And while the King
Said what he said, Tristram was seeing only
A last look in two dark and frightened eyes
That always in the moonlight would be shining,
Alone above the sound of Cornish waves
That always in the moonlight would be breaking
Cold upon Cornish rocks.

But occupation.
Like a neglected and insistent hound

Leaping upon his master's inattention,
Soon found him wearing on his younger shoulders
The yoke of a too mild and easy-trusting
And easy-futured king. He shaped and trained
An army that in time before would soon
Have made of Griffon a small anecdote
Hardly worth telling over after supper;
He built new ships and wharves, and razed old houses,
And so distressed a realm with renovation
Unsought and frowned on by slow denizens
For decades undisturbed, that many of them,
Viewing the visioned waste of a new hand,
Had wished him dead, or far from Brittany;
And for the flower of his activities,
He built a royal garden for Isolt
Of the white hands to bloom in, a white rose
Fairer than all fair roses in the world
Elsewhere—save one that was not white but dark,
Dark and love-red for ever, and not there,
Where the white rose was queen.

                                   So for two years
She reigned and waited, and there in her garden
Let rumor's noise, like thunder heard far off,

Rumble itself to silence and as nigh
To nothing as might be. But near the end
Of a long afternoon, alone with him,
She sat there watching Tristram, who in turn,
Still mystified at having in his care
To keep or crush, even as her father said,
So brave and frail a flower, sat watching her
With eyes that always had at least been kind,
If they had not said always everything
She would have had them say. Staring at him,
Like someone suddenly afraid of life,
She chilled him slowly with a question: "Tristram,"
She said, "what should I do were you to die?"

"Are there no prettier notions in your head
Than that?" said he, and made a task of laughing.
"There are no mortal purposes in me
Today, yet I may say what you would do:
Were I to die, you would live on without me.
But I would rather sing you an old song
Than die, and even for you, this afternoon."

"Yes, presently you will sing me an old song,"
She said. "It was a wonder seized me then

And made me ask like that what I should do
Were you to die. Were you to tire of me,
And go away from me and stay some time,
I should not die, for then you would come back.
You came back once, and you would come again;
For you would learn at last you needed me
More than all other creatures. But if you died,
Then you would not come back. What should I do
If you should go away and never come back?
I see almost a shadow on you sometimes,
As if there were some fearful thing behind you,
Not to be felt or seen—while you are here."

"I can feel only the sun behind me now—
Which is a fearful thing if we consider it
Too long, or look too long into its face."
Saying that, he smiled at her, not happily,
But rather as one who has left something out,
And gazed away over a vine-hung wall,
And over the still ocean where one ship
Was coming slowly in.

"If I lost you
For a long time," she said, with her insistence.

"I should not cry for what had come between,
For I should have you here with me again.
I am not one who must have everything.
I was not fated to have everything.
One may be wise enough, not having all,
Still to be found among the fortunate."

She stood beside him now and felt his arm
Closing around her like an arm afraid.
"Little you know, my child," he thought, in anguish
A moment for the fear and innocence
That he was holding and was his to hold,
"What ashes of all this wisdom might be left you
After one blast of sick reality
To tell the wise what words are to the heart."
And then aloud: "There's a ship coming in
From somewhere north of us."

                              "There are no ships
From the north now that are worth looking at,"
She said; and he could feel her trembling warm
Against him till he felt her scorching him
With an unconscious and accusing fire.
"There was a time when I was always gazing
[98]

North for a ship, but nothing is there now;
Or ships are all alike that are there now."

"They are not all like this one," Tristram said,
More to himself than to the white Isolt
Arming herself with blindness against fate,
"For there are trumpets blowing, as if a king
Were coming—and there's a dragon on the sail.
One of King Arthur's barges—by the Lord
In heaven, it is!—comes here to Brittany,
And for a cause that lives outside my knowledge.
Were this the King, we should have known of him."

"What does it mean?" she whispered; and her words
Wavered as if a terror not yet revealed
Had flown already inland from that ship.

"God knows," he said, "but it will not be long
Before we shall all know."   She followed him
Into her father's castle, where the new
Looked ancient now; and slowly, after silence,
He left her waiting there at the same window
Where she had waited for so long before,
When she was looking always to the north;

And having left her there, alone with wonder,
He went alone with wonder to the shore,
Where a gay ship was coming gaily in,
And saw descending from it soon, and gaily,
As always, Sir Gawaine from Camelot.

VI

Gawaıne, in Cornwall once, having seen Isolt
Of Ireland with her pallid mask of pride,
Which may have been as easy a mask as any,
He thought, for prisoned love and scorn to wear,
Had found in her dark way of stateliness
Perfection providentially not his
To die for. He recalled a wish to die,
But only as men healed remember pain;
And here in Tristram's garden, far from Cornwall,
Gawaine, musing upon this white Isolt
Of Brittany, whose beauty had heretofore,
For him, lived rather as that of a white name
Than of a living princess, found himself
Again with a preoccupied perfection
To contemplate. The more he contemplated,
The more he arraigned fate and wondered why
Tristram should be at odds with banishment,

Or why Tristram should care who banished him,
Or for how long, or for what violet eyes
And Irish pride and blue-black Irish hair
Soever. He smiled with injured loyalty
For Tristram in a banishment like this,
With a whole world to shine in save Cornwall,
And Cornwall the whole world; and if he sighed,
He may have sighed apart, and harmlessly,
Perceiving in this Isolt a continence
Too sure for even a fool to ponder twice,
A little for himself. They faced each other
On a stone bench with vine-leaves over them,
And flowers too many for them to see before them,
And trees around them with birds singing in them,
And God's whole gift of summer given in vain
For one who could feel coming in her heart
A longer winter than any Breton sun
Should ever warm away, and with it coming,
Could laugh to hear Gawaine making her laugh.

"I have been seeing you for some hours," he said,
"And I appraise you as all wonderful.
The longer I observe and scrutinize you,
[101]

The less do I become a king of words
To bring them into action. They retreat
And hide themselves, leaving me as I may
To make the best of a disordered remnant,
Unworthy of allegiance to your face
And all the rest of you. You are supreme
In a deceit that says fragility
Where there is nothing fragile. You have eyes
That almost weep for grief, seeing from heaven
How trivial and how tragic a small place
This earth is, and so make a sort of heaven
Where they are seen. Your hair, if shorn and woven,
The which may God forbid, would then become
A nameless cloth of gold whiter than gold,
Imprisoning light captured from paradise.
Your small ears are two necessary leaves
Of living alabaster never of earth,
Whereof the flower that is your face is made,
And is a paradisal triumph also—
Along with your gray eyes and your gold hair
That is not gold. Only God knows, who made it,
What color it is exactly. I don't know.
The rest of you I dare not estimate,

Saving your hands and feet, which authorize
A period of some leisure for the Lord
On high for their ineffable execution.
Your low voice tells how bells of singing gold
Would sound through twilight over silent water.
Yourself is a celestial emanation
Compounded of a whiteness and a warmth
Not yet so near to heaven, or far from it,
As not to leave men wiser for their dreams
And distances in apprehending you.
Your signal imperfection, probably,
Is in your peril of having everything,
And thereby overwhelming with perfection
A man who sees so much of it at once,
And says no more of it than I am saying.
I shall begin today to praise the Lord,
I think, for sparing an unworthy heart
An early wound that once might not have healed.
If there lives in me more than should be told,
Not for the world's last oyster would I tell it
To the last ear alive, surely not yours."

"If you were one of the last two alive,
The other might make of you the last," she said,

Laughing. "You are not making love to me,
Gawaine, and if you were it wouldn't matter.
Your words, and even with edges a bit worn
By this time, will do service for years yet.
You will not find that you have dulled them much
On me, and you will have them with you always."

"I don't know now whether I am or not,"
Said he, "and say with you it wouldn't matter.
For Tristram, off his proper suavity,
Has fervor to slice whales; and I, from childhood,
Have always liked this world. No, I should say
That I was covering lightly under truth
A silent lie that may as well be silent;
For I can see more care than happiness
In those two same gray eyes that I was praising."

"Gawaine," she said, turning the same gray eyes
On his and holding them, with hers half laughing,
"Your fame is everywhere alike for lightness,
And I am glad that you have not my heart
To be a burden for you on too long
A journey, where you might find hearts of others

Not half so burdensome. Do you like that?
If you do not, say it was never said,
And listen as if my words were bells of gold,
Or what you will. You will be hanged some day
For saying things, and I shall not be there
To save you, saying how little you meant by them.
You may be lighter than even your enemies
Would see you in their little scales of envy,
Yet in your lightness, if I'm not a fool,
There lives a troubled wonder for a few
You care for. Now if two of them were here,
Would you say what was best, in your reflection,
And on your honor say no more of it,
For one of them alone here to believe
When Tristram goes with you to Camelot?
While he is there, King Arthur, it appears,
Will make of him a Knight of the Round Table—
All which would be illustrious and delightful
Enough for me, if that were to be all.
And though the world is in our confidence,
Your honor as a man will forget that;
And you will answer, wisely perhaps, or not,
One question, which in brief is only this:

What right name should an innocence like mine
Deserve. if I believed he would come back?"
She watched him with expectant eyes, wherefrom
The ghost of humor suddenly had vanished.

Gawaine, who felt a soreness at his heart
That he had seldom felt there for another
Before, and only briefly for himself,
Felt also a cloud coming in his eyes.
"I can see only one thing to believe,"
He said, believing almost he could see it,
"And that is, he will come—as he must come.
Why should he not come back again, for you?
Who in this world would not come back, for you!
God's life, dear lady, why should he not come back?"
He cried, and with a full sincerity
Whereat she closed her eyes and tried to speak,
Despairingly, with pale and weary lips
That would not speak until she made them speak.

"Gawaine," she said, "you are not fooling me;
And I should be a fool if hope remained
Within me that you might be. You know truth

As well as I do. He will not come back.
King Mark will kill him." For so long unspoken,
She had believed those words were tamed in her
Enough to be released and to return
To the same cage there in her aching heart
Where they had lived and fought since yesterday.
But when she felt them flying away from her,
And heard them crying irretrievably
Between her and Gawaine, and everywhere,
Tears followed them until she felt at last
The touch of Gawaine's lips on her cold fingers,
Kindly and light.

     "No, Mark will hardly kill him,"
He told her. Breathing hard and hesitating,
He waited as a felon waits a whip,
And went on with a fluent desperation:
"Mark is in prison now—for forgery
Of the Pope's name, by force of which Tristram
Was to go forth to fight the Saracens,
And by safe inference to find a grave
Not far ahead. Impossible, if you like,
And awkward out of all ineptitude,

And clumsy beyond credence, yet the truth,—
As the impossible so often is.
In his unwinking hate he saw Tristram
Too near for easy vengeance, and so blundered
Into the trap that has him. This was not
For me to tell, and it is not for you,
Upon your royal honor as a woman
Of honor more than royal to reveal.
Mercy compels me to forego my word
And to repeat the one right thing for you
In reason to believe. He will come back;
And you, if you are wise—and you are that
Beyond the warrant of your sheltered years—
Will find him wiser in his unworthiness,
And worthier of your wisdom and your love,
When this wild fire of what a man has not
Reveals at last, in embers all gone out,
That which he had, and has, and may have always,
To prize aright thereafter and to pray for.
Out of my right I talk to you like this,
And swear by heaven, since I have gone so far,
That your worst inference here is not my knowledge.
He may come back at once. If otherwise—well,

He will come back with a new vision in him
And a new estimation of God's choice.
I have told you what neither grief nor guile
Would of themselves alone have wrung from me.
The rest will be in you, you being yourself."

"Yes, you have thrown your offices away
And you have left your honor for me to keep,"
She said, and pressed his hands in gratitude.
"Here it will be as safe as in the sea.
I thank you, and believe you.   Leave me here
Alone, to think; to think—and to believe."
She brushed her eyes and tried as if to smile,
But had no smile in answer.   For Gawaine,
Infrequently in earnest, or sincere
To conscious inconvenience, was in love,
Or thought he was, and would enjoy alone,
Without a smile and as he might, the first
Familiar pangs of his renunciation.

He wandered slowly downward to the shore
Where he found Tristram, gazing at the ship
Which in the morning would be taking them
Together away from Brittany and Isolt

Of the white hands to England, where **Tristram,**
A knight only of Mark's investiture
Today, would there be one of the Round Table—
So long the symbol of a world in order,
Soon to be overthrown by love and fate
And loyalty forsworn. Had Gawaine then
Beheld a cloud that was not yet in sight,
There would have been more sorrow in his eyes
For time ahead of him than for time now,
Or for himself. But where he saw no cloud
That might not be dissolved, and so in time
Forgotten, there was no sorrow in his eyes
For time to come that would be longer coming,
To him, than for the few magnanimous days
Of his remembrance of enforced eclipse.

"Tristram," he said, "why in the name of God
Are you not looking at your garden now,
And why are you not in it with your wife?
I left her, after making love to her
With no progression of effect whatever,
More than to make her laugh at me, and then
To make her cry for you for going away.

I said you would be coming back at once,
And while I said it I heard pens in heaven
Scratching a doubtful evidence against me."

Tristram, in indecision between anger
Deserving no indulgence and surprise
Requiring less, scowled and laughed emptily:
"Gawaine, if you were any one else alive
I might not always be at home to you,
Or to your bland particularities.
Why should a wedded exile hesitate
In his return to his own wife and garden?
I know the picture that your folly draws
Of woe that is awaiting me in Cornwall.
But we are going to Camelot, not to Cornwall.
King Mark, with all his wealth of hate for me,
Is not so rich and rotten and busy with it
As to be waiting everywhere at once
To see me coming. He waits most in Cornwall,
Preferring for mixed reasons of his own
Not frequently to shine far out of it."

"He may not be so rotten as some whose names
Have fallen from my deciduous memory,"

Gawaine said, with a shrug of helplessness,
"But all the same, with Mark and his resource
In England, your best way's away from there
As early and expeditiously as may be.
Mark's arm is not the only arm he uses;
My fear for you is not my only fear.
Fear for yourself in you may be as nothing,
Which is commendable and rather common
In Camelot, as fellows who read and write
Are not so rare there that we crown them for it.
But there's a fear more worthy than no fear,
And it may be the best inheritance
Of luckless ones with surer sight than yours,
And with perception more prophetical
Than yours. I say this hoping it will hurt,
But not offend. You see how lax I am
When I'm away from royal discipline,
And how forgetful of unspoken caution
I am when I'm afraid to be afraid.
I thrust my head into the lion's mouth,
And if my head comes off, it will have done,
For once if only once, the best it might.
I doubt if there's a man with eyes and ears

Who is more sadly and forlornly certain
Of what another's wisdom—born of weakness,
Like all born mortal attributes and errors—
Is like to leave behind it of itself
In you, when you have heard and hated it,
But all the same, Tristram, if I were you,
I'd sail away for Camelot tomorrow,
And there be made a Knight of the Round Table;
And then, being then a Knight of the Round Table,
I should come back. I should come back at once.
Now let the lion roar."

                    He laid his hands
On Tristram's iron shoulders, which he felt
Shaking under his touch, and with a smile
Of unreturned affection walked away
In silence to the ship. Tristram, alone,
Moved heavily along the lonely shore,
To seat himself alone upon a rock
Where long waves had been rolling in for ages,
And would be rolling when no man or woman
Should know or care to know whether or not
Two specks of life, in time so far forgotten

As in remembrance never to have been,
Were Tristram and Isolt—Isolt in Cornwall.
Isolt of the wild frightened violet eyes,
Isolt and her last look, Isolt of Ireland.
Alone, he saw the slanting waves roll in,
Each to its impotent annihilation
In a long wash of foam, until the sound
Become for him a warning and a torture,
Like a malign reproof reiterating
In vain its cold and only sound of doom.
Then he arose, with his eyes gazing still
Into the north, till with his face turned inland
He left the crested wash of those long waves
Behind him to fall always on that sand,
And to sound always that one word—"Isolt."

As if in undesigned obedience
To Gawaine's admonition, he went idly
And blindly back to the sun-flooded garden
Where sat the white Isolt whose name was not
The name those waves, unceasing and unheard,
Were sounding where they fell. Still as Gawaine
Had left her, Tristram found her. She looked up

With a wan light of welcome flashing sadly
To see him; and he knew that such a light
As that could shine for him only from eyes
Where tears had been before it.   They were not
There now, and there was now no need of them
To make him ask, in a self-smiting rage
Of helpless pity, if such a love as hers
Might not unshared be nearer to God's need,
In His endurance of a blinder Fate,
Than a love shared asunder, but still shared,
By two for doom elected and withheld
Apart for time to play with.   Once he had seen,
Imploring it, the light of a far wisdom
Tingeing with hope the night of time between,
But there was no light now.   There might be peace,
Awaiting them where they were done with time—
Time for so long disowning both of them,
And slowly the soul first, saving the rest
To mock the soul—but there was no peace now.
When there was no time left for peace on earth,
After farewells and vestiges forgotten,
There might be time enough for peace somewhere;
But that was all far off, and in a darkness

Blacker than any night that ever veiled
A stormy chaos of the foaming leagues
That roared unseen between him and Cornwall.

All this was in his mind, as it was there
Always, if not thought always, when she spoke:
"Tristram, you are not angry or distressed
If I am not so happy here today
As you have seen me here before sometimes,
And may see me again. Tomorrow morning
If I am here, I shall be here alone.
I wonder for how long."

      "For no day longer
Than I'm away," he said, and held her face
Between his hands. "Then, if you like, my child,
Your wonder may come after your surprise
That I should come so soon. There's no long voyage
From here to Camelot, and I've no long fear
King Arthur will engage himself for ever
In making me a Knight of the Round Table.
King Mark . . ."

      "And why do you mention him to me!"
She cried, forgetful of her long command

Of what she had concealed and stifled from him.,
"I should have said King Mark was the last name
Of all, or all but one, that I should hear
From you today. Were there no better days!"

"King Mark says I'm a knight, but not King Arthur—
Not yet—was all that I was going to say;
And I am not saying that because I love him--
Only that you should hear the difference
From me, and have at least some joy of it.
I shall not feel Mark's sword upon my shoulder
Again until I feel the edge of it;
And that will not befall in Camelot,
Or wheresoever I shall carry with me
One of these arms that are not useless yet."

"And where do you plan next to carry them
To prove yourself a Knight of the Round Table?"
She said, and with a flame filling her eyes
As if a soul behind them were on fire.
"What next one among thieves, with Griffon gone,
Will be the nearest to your heart's desire?"

If her lip curled a little in asking that,
Tristram was looking down and did not see it.

"Where do I plan to carry my two arms
Away with me from Camelot, do you ask?
My purpose is to bring them here with me
To Brittany—both of them, God willing so.
You are not here with me, but in the past
This afternoon, and that's not well for you.
When I'm an exile, as you know I am,
Where would your fancy drive me, if not here?
All that was long ago."

    "So long ago,
Tristram, that you have lived for nothing else
Than for a long ago that follows you
To sleep, and has a life as long as yours.
Sometimes I wish that heaven had let you have her,
And given me back all that was left of you,
To teach and heal. I might be sure of that.
Or, to be sure of nothing, if only sure,
Would be a better way for both of us
Than to be here together as we have been
Since Gawaine came from Cornwall in that ship."

"From Cornwall? Are you dreaming when you say it?"
He questioned her as if he too were dreaming
[118]

That she had said it; and his heart was cold.
"From Cornwall? Did you not hear Gawaine saying
That he had come for me from Camelot?
Do you see Arthur, who loves Mark almost
As hard as I do, sending ships for me
From Cornwall? If you can see things like that,
You are seeing more of that which never was
Than will be needful where we need so much
Right seeing to see ourselves. If we see others,
Let us, for God's sake, see them where they are—
Not where they were. The past, or part of it,
Is dead—or we that would be living in it
Had best be dead. Why do you say to me
That Gawaine came from Cornwall in that ship?"

There was another gleam now in her eyes
Than yesterday had been imaginable
For Tristram, even had he been strangling her
In some imagined madness. "What?" she said;
"Did I say Cornwall? If I did, perhaps
It was because I thought the sound of it
Would make you happy. So far as I'm aware,
You have not heard that name in a long time.

Did I say Cornwall? If I did, forgive me.
I should have said that I said Camelot.
Not the same place at all."

                                    Dimly alive
To knowledge of a naked heart before him,
For him to soothe and comfort with cold lies,
He knew that lies could have no cooling virtue,
Even though they might be falling on this heart
As fast and unregarded as rain falls
Upon an angry sea. Anger so new,
And unforetold, was hardly to be known
At first for what it was, or recognized
With more than silence. If he recognized it,
Before him in a garden full of sunshine,
He saw it as a shadow in the night
Between him and two dark and frightened eyes
And the last look that he had seen in them,
With music shrieking always in the moonlight
Above him, and below him the long sound
Of Cornish waves that would be sounding always,
Foaming on those cold rocks. For a long time
He saw not the white face accusing him,

And heard no sound that others might have heard
Where there was once a garden for Isolt—
Isolt of the white hands, who said no more
To him that afternoon. He left her there,
And like a man who was no longer there,
He stared over the wall, and over water
Where sunlight flashed upon a million waves,
Only to see through night, and through moonlight,
The coming after of a darker night
Than he could see, and of a longer night
Than there was time to fear. Assured of nothing,
He was too sure of all to tell more lies
In idle mercy to an angry woman
Whose unavailing alchemy of hope
No longer, or not now, found love in pity.

But with no more display of desolation
Than any one's wife among a thousand wives
Might then have made, foreseeing nothing worse
Than to be left alone for no long time,
She met him without anger in the morning,
And in the morning said farewell to him,
With trumpets blowing and hundreds cheering him:

And from a moving shore she waved at him
One of her small white hands, and smiled at him.
That all should see her smiling when he sailed
Away from her for Camelot that morning.
Gawaine, recovered early from a wound
Within a soon-recuperating heart,
Waved a gay hat on board for two gray eyes
On shore; and as the ship went farther out,
The sound of trumpets blowing golden triumph
Rang faintly and more faintly as it went,
Farther and always farther, till no sound
Was heard, and there was nothing to be seen
But a ship sailing always to the north,
And slowly showing smaller to the sight.

She watched again from the same window now
Where she had watched and waited for so long
For the slow coming of another ship
That came at last. What other ship was coming,
And after what long time and change, if ever,
No seer or wizard of the future knew,
She thought, and Tristram least of all. Far off,
The ship was now a speck upon the water,

And soon, from where she was, would not be that,
And soon was not; and there was nothing left
That day, for her, in the world anywhere,
But white birds always flying, and still flying,
And always the white sunlight on the sea.

VII

Isolt alone with time, Isolt of Ireland,
So candid and exact in her abhorrence
Of Mark that she had driven him in defeat
To favors amiable if unillusioned,
Saw, with a silent love consuming her,
A silent hate inhibiting in Mark
A nature not so base as it was common,
And not so cruel as it was ruinous
To itself and all who thwarted it.   Wherefore,
Tristram it was, Tristram alone, she knew,
That he would see alive in useless fire,
Thereafter to be haunted all his days
By vengeance unavenging.   Where was vengeance
For the deforming wounds of difference
That fate had made and hate would only canker,
And death corrupt in him till he should die?

But this was not for Mark, and she said little
To Mark of more than must in ceremony
Be said, perforce, fearing him to misread
Her deprecating pity for his birthright
For the first meltings of renunciation,
Where there was none to melt. — "If I'm so fair,
Why then was all this comely merchandise
Not sold as colts are, in a market-place,"
She asked herself. "Then Tristram could have bought me,
Whether he feared my love was hate or not,
And whether or not he killed my uncle Morhaus."
And there were days when she would make Brangwaine
Go over the bridge and into the woods with her
To cheer her while she thought.—"If I were Queen
In this forsaken land," Brangwaine said once,
"I'd give three bags of gold to three strong men,
And let them sew King Mark into a sack,
And let them sink him into the dark sea
On a dark night, and Andred after him.
So doing, I'd welcome Erebus, and so leave
This world a better place."—"If you sew Andred
Into a sack, I'll do the rest myself,
And give you more than your three bags of gold,"

Isolt said; and a penitential laugh
Tempered an outburst that was unrepeated—
Though for a year, and almost a year after,
Brangwaine had waited. But Isolt would laugh
For her no more. The fires of love and fear
Had slowly burned away so much of her
That all there was of her, she would have said,
Was only a long waiting for an end
Of waiting—till anon she found herself,
Still waiting, where a darkening eastern sea
Made waves that in their sound along the shore
Told of a doom that was no longer fear.

Incredulous after Lancelot's departure
From Joyous Gard, Tristram, alone there now,
With a magnificence and a mystery
More to be felt than seen among the shadows
Around him and behind him, saw the ocean
Before him from the window where he stood,
And seeing it heard the sound of Cornish foam
So far away that he must hear it always
On the world's end that was for him in Cornwall
A forest-hidden sunset filled long clouds

Eastward over the sea with a last fire,
Dim fire far off, wherein Tristram beheld
Tintagel slowly smouldering in the west
To a last darkness, while on Cornish rocks
The moan of Cornish water foamed and ceased
And foamed again. Pale in a fiery light,
With her dark hair and her dark frightened eyes,
And their last look at him, Isolt of Ireland
Above him on the stairs, with only a wall
Waist-high between her and her last escape,
Stood watching there for him who was not there.
He could feel all those endless evening leagues
Of England foiling him and mocking him
From where it was too late for him to go,
And where, if he were there, coming so late,
There would be only darkness over death
To meet his coming while she stood alone
By the dark wall, with dark fire hiding her,
Waiting—for him. She would not be there long;
She must die there in that dark fire, or fall,
Throwing herself away on those cold rocks
Where there was peace, or she must come to him
Over those western leagues, mysteriously

Defeating time and place. She might do so
If she were dead, he thought, and were a ghost,
As even by now she might be, and her body,
Where love would leave so little of earth to burn,
Might even by now be burning. So, as a ghost
It was that she would have to come to him,
On little feet that he should feel were coming.
She would be dead, but there might be no pain
In that for him when the first death of knowing
That she was dead was ended, and he should know
She had found rest. She would come back to him
Sometimes, and touch him in the night so lightly
That he might see her between sleep and waking,
And see that last look in her eyes no more—
For it would not be there.

                    It was not there.
Woman or ghost, her last look in the moonlight
Was not in her eyes now. Softly, behind him,
The coming of her steps had made him turn
To see there was no fear in her eyes now;
And whether she had come to him from death,
Or through those dark and heavy velvet curtains,

She had come to him silent and alone,
And as the living come—living or not.
Whether it was a warm ghost he was holding,
Or a warm woman, or a dream of one,
With tear-filled eyes in a slow twilight shining
Upward and into his, only to leave him
With eyes defeated of all sight of her,
Was more than he dared now let fate reveal.
Whatever it was that he was holding there,
Woman or ghost or dream, was not afraid;
And the warm lips that pressed themselves again
On his, and held them there as if to die there,
Were not dead now. The rest might be illusion—
Camelot, Arthur, Guinevere, Gawaine,
Lancelot, and that voyage with Lancelot
To Joyous Gard, this castle by the sea—
The sea itself, and the clouds over it,
Like embers of a day that like a city
Far off somewhere in time was dying alone,
Slowly, in fire and silence—the fading light
Around them, and the shadowy room that held them—
All these,—if they were shadows, let them be so,
He thought. But let these two that were not shadows

Be as they were, and live—by time no more
Divided until time for them should cease.
They were not made for time as others were,
And time therefore would not be long for them
Wherein for love to learn that in their love,
Where fate was more than time and more than love,
Time never was, save in their fear of it—
Fearing, as one, to find themselves again
Intolerably as two that were not there.

Isolt, to see him, melted slowly from him,
Moving as if in motion, or in much thought,
All this might vanish and the world go with it.
Still in his arms, and sure that she was there,
She smiled at him as only joy made wise
By sorrow smiles at fear, as if a smile
Would teach him all there was for life to know,
Or not to know. Her dark and happy eyes
Had now a darkness in them that was light;
There was no longer any fear in them,
And there was no fear living on a face
That once, too fair for beauty to endure
Without the jealous graving of slow pain.

Was now, for knowledge born of all endurance,
Only beyond endurance beautiful
With a pale fire of love where shone together
Passion and comprehension beyond being
For any long time; and while she clung to him,
Each was a mirror for the other there
Till tears of vision and of understanding
Were like a mist of wisdom in their eyes,
Lest in each other they might see too soon
All that fate held for them when Guinevere,
In a caprice of singularity
Seizing on Mark's unsafe incarceration,
Made unrevealed a journey to Cornwall,
Convoyed by two attendant eminent leeches
Who found anon the other fairest woman
Alive no longer like to stay alive
Than a time-tortured and precarious heart,
Long wooed by death, might or might not protest.
All which being true, Guinevere gave herself
Humbly to God for telling him no lies;
And Lancelot gave his conscience to God also,
As he had given it once when he had felt
The world shake as he gave it. Stronger than God,

When all was done the god of love was fate,
Where all was love. And this was in a darkness
Where time was always dying and never dead,
And where God's face was never to be seen
To tell the few that were to lose the world
For love how much or little they lost for it,
Or paid with others' pain.

                    "Isolt! Isolt!"
He murmured, as if struggling to believe
That one name, and one face there in the twilight,
Might for a moment, or a moment longer,
Defeat oblivion. How could she be with him
When there were all those western leagues of twilight
Between him and Cornwall? She was not there
Until she spoke:

                    "Tristram!" was all she said;
And there was a whole woman in the sound
Of one word surely spoken. She was there,
Be Cornwall where it was or never was,
And England all a shadow on the sea
That was another shadow, and on time

That was one shadow more. If there was death
Descending on all this, and this was love,
Death then was only another shadow's name;
And there was no more fear in Tristram's heart
Of how she fared, and there was no more pain.
God must have made it so, if it was God—
Or death, if it was death. If it was fate,
There was a way to be made terribly
For more than time, yet one that each knew well,
And said well, silently, would not be long.
How long now mattered nothing, and what there was
Was all.

          "Tristram!" She said again his name,
And saying it she could feel against herself
The strength of him all trembling like a tower
Long shaken by long storms, in darkness far
From hers, where she had been alone with it
Too long for longer fear. But that was nothing,
For that was done, and they were done with time.
It was so plain that she could laugh to see it;
And almost laughing she looked up at him,
And said once more, "Tristram!"

                                        She felt herself
Smothered and crushed in a forgetful strength
Like that of an incredulous blind giant,
Seizing amain on all there was of life
For him, and all that he had said was lost.
She waited, and he said, "Isolt! Isolt!"
He that had spoken always with a word
To spare, found hungrily that only one
Said all there was to say, till she drew more
From him and he found speech.

                                    "There are no kings
Tonight," he told her, with at last a smile,
"To make for you another prison of this—
Or none like one in Cornwall. These two arms
Are prison enough to keep you safe in them
So long as they are mine."

                                    "They are enough,
Tristram," she said. "All the poor kings and queens
Of time are nothing now. They are all gone
Where shadows go, after the sun goes down.
The last of them are far away from here,

And you and I are here alone together.
We are the kings and queens of everything;
And if we die, nothing can alter that,
Or say it was not so. Before we die,
Tell me how many lives ago it was
I left you in the moonlight on those stairs,
And went up to that music and those voices,
And for God's reason then did not go mad!
Tell me how old the world was when it died—
For I have been alone with time so long
That time and I are strangers. My heart knows
That I was there too long, but knows not yet
Why I was there, or why so many alive
Are as they are. They are not with me here.
They all went when the world went. You and I
Only are left, waiting alone for God—
Down here where the world was!"

                                    Fire in her eyes,
And twilight on her warm dark-waving hair
And on a warm white face too beautiful
To be seen twice alive and still be found
Alive and white and warm and the same face,

Compelled him with her pallid happiness
To see where life had been so long the fuel
Of love, that for a season he saw nothing,
Save a still woman somewhere in a moonlight,
Where there were stairs and lamps and a cold sound
That waves made long ago. Yet she was warm
There in his arms, and she was not the ghost
He feared she was, chilling him first with doubt.

"We are the last that are alive, Isolt,
Where the world was. Somewhere surrounding us
There are dim shapes of men with many names,
And there are women that are made of mist,
Who may have names and faces. If I see them,
They are too far away for you to see.
They all went when the world went. You are the world,
Isolt—you are the world!"

"Whatever I am,
You are the last alive to make me listen
While you say that. You are the world, Tristram.
My worth is only what it is to you.
In Cornwall I was not appraised unduly,
Save as a queen to garnish, when essential,

A court where almost anything with a face
Would have been queen enough. And you know best
How much I was a queen. The best I know
Is all there is to know—that some command
In heaven, or some imperial whim of mercy
Brought Guinevere to Cornwall, and brought me
Here to this place that may be real sometime,
And to your arms that must be real indeed.
Let them be real! . . . O God, Tristram! Tristram!
Where are those blindfold years that we have lost
Because a blind king bought of a blind father
A child blinder than they? She might have drawn
A knife across her throat rather than go! . . .
But no—had she done that, she would have died;
And all her seeming needlessness alive
Would have been all it seemed. Oh, it would be
A fearful thing for me to close my eyes
Too long, and see too much that is behind me!
When they were open you might not be here.
Your arms that hold me now might not be yours,
But those of a strong monster and a stranger.
Make me believe again that you are here! . . .
Yes, you are here!"

　　　　　　　　All her firm litheness melted
Into the sure surrender of a child
When she said that; and her dark eyes became
For a dim moment gray, and were like eyes
That he had left behind in Brittany.
Another moment, and they were dark again,
And there was no such place as Brittany.
Brittany must have died when the world died—
The world, and time. He had forgotten that,
Till he found now, insensibly almost,
How soft and warm and small so proud a queen
As this Isolt could be. Dimly deceived
By the dark surety of her stateliness
And by the dark indignity of distance,
His love may not have guessed how this Isolt
Of Ireland, with her pride that frightened kings.
Should one day so ineffably become
So like a darker child for him to break
Or save, with a word hushed or a word spoken;
And so his love may well never have seen
How surely it was fate that his love now
Should light with hers at the last fire of time
A flaming way to death. Fire in her eyes,

And sorrow in her smile, foretold unsaid
More than he saw.

     "You are not sad that heaven
Should hide us here together, God knows how long,
And surely are not fearful," he said, smiling.
"Before there was a man or woman living,
It was all chronicled with nights and days
That we should find each other tonight like this,
There was no other way for love like ours
To be like this than always to have been.
Your love that I see looking into mine
Might have in it a shining of more knowledge
Than love needs to be wise; and love that's wise
Will not say all it means. Untimely words,
Where love and wisdom are not quarrelling,
Are good words not to say."

      "If you see wisdom
Shining out of my eyes at you sometime,
Say it is yours, not mine. Untimely words
Are not for love, and are like frost on flowers
Where love is not for long. When we are done

With time, Tristram, nothing can be for long.
You would know that if you had been a woman
Alone in Cornwall since those lights went out,
And you went down those stairs. Sometime I'll ask
How far you wandered and what rainy end
There ever was to that unending night,
But now I shall not ask an answer more
Of you than this, or more of God than this;
For this is all—no matte· for how long.
Do not forget, my love, that once Isolt
Said that; and wheresoever she may be then,
See her where she is now—alone with you,
And willing enough to be alone in heaven—
Or hell, if so it be—and let you live
Down here without her for a thousand years,
Were that the way of happiness for you,
Tristram. So long as fate itself may find
No refuge or concealment or escape
From heaven for me save in some harm for you.
I shall not be unhappy after this."

"He that pays all for all is past all harm,"
He said, "I can forgive your thousand years,

And you are sorry for them. The one harm
Deserving a fantastic apprehension
Is one that surely cannot come tonight.
Only an army of infernal men—
And they would not be men—will find a way
Over these walls, or through them, to find me—
Or you, tonight. Untimely words again,
But only as a folly to match yours
In feigning harm for me. Dear God in heaven!
If one such reptile thought inhabited
A nature that was never mine before,
Some woman at hand should watch you properly
While I, like Judas, only running faster,
Might hang myself."

      He felt her body throbbing
As if it held a laugh buried alive,
And suddenly felt all his eloquence
Hushed with her lips. Like a wild wine her love
Went singing through him and all over him;
And like a warning her warm loveliness
Told him how far away it would all be
When it was warm no longer. For some time

He was a man rather by dread possessed
Than by possession, when he found again
That he was listening to the blended gold
And velvet that was always in her voice:

"Your meditations are far wanderers,
And you must have them all home before dark;
Or I shall find myself at work to learn
What's in me so to scatter them.   Dear love,
If only you had more fear for yourself
You might, for caution, be my cause for less.
My cage is empty, and I'm out of it;
And you and I are in another cage—
A golden cage—together.   Reason it is,
Not fear, that lets me know so much as that;
Also, the while you care not for yourself
Where shadows are, there are things always walking.
Meanwhile your fear for me has been a screen
Of distance between me and my destruction—
Mine, love, and yours.   Fears are not always blind.
If love be blind, mine has been so for watching
Too long across an empty world for you;
And if it be myself now that is blind,

I may still hide myself somewhere alone—
Somewhere away from you.   Whatever we are,
We are not so blind that we are not to know
The darkness when it comes, if it must come.
We are not children teasing little waves
To follow us along a solid shore.
I see a larger and a darker tide,
Somewhere, than one like that.   But where and when,
I do not wish to see."

                      "If love that's blind,"
He said, holding her face and gazing at it,
"Sees only where a tide that's dark and large
May be somewhere sometime, love that has eyes
Will fix itself, and with a nearer wonder,
Upon Isolt—who is enough to see.
Isolt alone.   All else that emulates
And envies her—black faggots in red flame,
A sunshine slanting into a dark forest,
A moonlight on white foam along black ledges,
Sunlight and rain, trees twinkling after rain,
Panthers and antelopes, children asleep—
All these are native elsewhere, and for now

[142]

Are not important. Love that has eyes to see
Sees now only Isolt. Isolt alone.
Isolt, and a few stars."

                              "Were I the shadow
Of half so much as this that you are seeing
Of me, I should not be Isolt of Ireland,
Or any Isolt alive. All you can see
Of me is only what the Lord accomplished
When he made me for love. When he made you
His love remembered that; and whether or not
His way was the most merciful, he knows—
Not we. Or was it fate, stronger than all?
A voice within me says that God, seeing all,
Was more compassionate than to let love see
Too far—loving his world too well for that.
We do not have to know—not yet. The flower
That will have withered from the world for ever
With us, will die sometime; and when it fades,
And dies, and goes, we shall have gone already,
And it will all be done. If I go first,
No fear of your forgetting shall attend me,
Leaving with you the mind and heart of love—

The love that knows what most it will remember.
If I lose you, I shall not have to wait—
Not long.   There will be only one thing then
Worth waiting for.   No, I shall not wait long . . .
I have said that.   Now listen, while I say this:
My life to me is not a little thing;
It is a fearful and a lovely thing;
Only my love is more."

                        "God knows," he said,
"How far a man may be from his deserving
And yet be fated for the undeserved.
I might, were I the lord of your misgivings,
Be worthier of them for destroying them;
And even without the mightiness in me
For that, I'll tell you, for your contemplation,
Time is not life.   For many, and many more,
Living is mostly for a time not dying—
But not for me.   For me, a few more years
Of shows and slaughters, or the tinsel seat
Of a small throne, would not be life.   Whatever
It is that fills life high and full, till fate
Itself may do no more, it is not time.
Years are not life."

"'I have not come so far
To learn," she said, and shook her head at him,
"What years are, for I know. Years are not life;
Years are the shells of life, and empty shells
When they hold only days, and days, and days.
God knows if I know that—so let it pass.
Let me forget; and let me ask you only
Not to forget that all your feats at arms,
Your glamour that is almost above envy,
Your strength and eminence and everything,
Leave me a woman still—a one-love woman,
Meaning a sort of ravenous one-child mother,
Whose one-love pictures in her composition
Panthers and antelopes, children asleep,
And all sorts of engaging animals
That most resemble a much-disordered queen,
Her crown abandoned and her hair in peril,
And she herself a little deranged, no doubt,
With too much happiness. Whether he lives
Or dies for her, he tells her is no matter,
Wherefore she must obediently believe him.
All he would ask of her would be as easy
As hearing waves, washing the shore down there

For ever, and believing herself drowned.
In seeing so many of her, he might believe her
To be as many at once as drops of rain;
Perhaps a panther and a child asleep
At the same time."

                         He saw dark laughter sparkling
Out of her eyes, but only until her face
Found his, and on his mouth a moving fire
Told him why there was death, and what lost song
Ulysses heard, and would have given his hands
And friends to follow and to die for. Slowly,
At last, the power of helplessness there was
In all that beauty of hers that was for him,
Breathing and burning there alone with him,
Until it was almost a part of him,
Suffused his passion with a tenderness
Attesting a sealed certainty not his
To cozen or wrench from fate, and one withheld
In waiting mercy from oblivious eyes—
His eyes and hers, that over darker water,
Where darker things than shadows would be coming,
Saw now no more than more stars in the sky.

He felt her throbbing softly in his arms,
And held her closer still—with half a fear
Returning that she might not be Isolt,
And might yet vanish where she sat with him,
Leaving him there alone, with only devils
Of hell supplanting her.

                        "Leave me the stars
A little longer," said Isolt. "In Cornwall,
So much alone there with them as I was,
One sees into their language and their story.
They must be more than fire; and if the stars
Are more than fire, what else is there for them
To be than love? I found all that myself;
For when a woman is left too much alone,
Sooner or later she begins to think;
And no man knows what then she may discover."

"Whether she be in Cornwall, or not there,
A woman driven to thinking of the stars
Too hard is in some danger," he said, sighing,
"Of being too much alone wherever she is."

Her face unseen, she smiled, hearing him sigh—
So much as if all patient chivalry

Were sighing with him. "One alone too long
In Cornwall has to think somewhat," she said,
"Or one may die. One may do worse than die.
If life that comes of love is more than death,
Love must be more than death and life together."

"Whether I know that life is more or not
Than death," he said, "I swear, with you for witness
You and the stars—that love is more than either."

"If I should have to answer twice to that,
I should not let myself be here with you
Tonight, with all the darkness I see coming
On land and over water." Then she ceased,
And after waiting as one waits in vain
For distant voices that are silent, "Tell me!"
She cried, seizing him hard and gazing at him,
"Tell me if I should make you go away!
I'm not myself alone now, and the stars
All tell me so."

He plucked her clinging hands
From his arms gently, and said, holding them,

"You cannot make me go away from you,
Isolt, for I believe, with you to tell me,
All your stars say. But never mind what they **say**
Of shadows coming. They are always coming—
Coming and going like all things but one.
Love is the only thing that in its being
Is what it seems to be. Glory and gold,
And all the rest, are weak and hollow staves
For even the poor to lean on. We know that—
We that have been so poor while grinning hinds
And shining wenches with all crowns to laugh at,
Have envied us, know that. Yet while you see
So many things written for you in starry fire,
Somehow you fear that I may lose my vision
Not seeing them. I shall not be losing it—
Not even in seeing beyond where you have seen.
Yes, I have seen your stars. You are the stars!
You are the stars when they all sing together.
You live, you speak, and you have not yet vanished.
You are Isolt—or I suppose you are!"

He was not sure of her not vanishing
Until he felt her tears, and her **warm arms**
[149]

Holding him with a sudden strength of love
That would have choked him had it not been **love.**
Each with unyielding lips refused the other
Language unasked; and their forgotten ears
Knew only as a murmur not remembered
A measured sea that always on the sand
Unseen below them, where time's only word
Was told in foam along a lonely shore,
Poured slowly its unceasing sound of doom—
Unceasing and unheard, and still unheard,
As with an imperceptible surrender
They moved and found each other's eyes again,
Burning away the night between their faces.

"Sometimes I fear that I shall fear for you
No more," she said; and to his ears her words
Were shaken music. "Why should I fear for you,
Or you for me, where nothing of earth is left,
Nothing of earth or time, that is worth fearing?
Sometimes I wonder if we are not like leaves
That have been blown by some warm wind of heaven
Far from the tree of life, still to be living
Here between life and death."

　　　　　　　　　　　　　　　"Why do those two
Vainglorious and abysmal little words
Pursue you and torment your soul?" said he.
"They are the serpents and uncertainties
That coil and rustle tonight among your fears,
Only because your fears have given to them
A shape without a substance.   Life and death?
Do not believe your stars if they are saying
That any such words are in their language now.
Whenever they tell you they are made of love,
Believe it; and forget them when they tell you
Of this or that man's living a thousand years.
Why should he wish to live a thousand years?
Whether your stars are made of love or fire,
There is a love that will outshine the stars.
There will be love when there are no more stars.
Never mind what they say of darkness coming
That may come sometime, or what else they say
Of terrors hidden in words like life and death.
What do they mean?   Never mind what they mean'
We have lived and we have died, and are alone
Where the world has no more a place for us,
Or time a fear for us, or death . . . Isolt!"

Her lips again had hushed him, and her name,
As when first he had found her in his arms,
Was all there was to say till he was saying
Muffled and husky words that groped and faltered,
Half silenced in a darkness of warm hair:
"Whatever it is that brings us here tonight,
Never believe—never believe again—
Your fear for me was more than love.   Time lied,
If he said that.   When we are done with time,
There is no time for fear.   It was not fear—
It was love's other name.   Say it was that!
Say to me it was only one of time's lies!
Whatever it was—never mind what it was!
There will be time enough for me to die.
Never mind death tonight. . . . Isolt! Isolt!"

VIII

Albeit the sun was high, the breath of morning
Was in the trees where Tristram stood alone
With happiness, watching a bright summer sea
That like a field of heaving steel and silver
Flashed there below him, and as harmlessly
As if an ocean had no darker work

To do than flash, and was to bear thereafter
No other freight than light. Joy sang in him
Till he could sing for joy, and would have done so,
Had not the lowly fear that humbles princes
Constrained him and so hindered him from giving
A little too much to those who served and feared him,
And willingly would listen; wherefore, turning
Away from the white music the waves made,
He lost himself again in a small forest,
Admiring the new miracle of the leaves,
And hearing, if one bird sang, as many as ten.
Now he could see once more the walls and towers
Of Joyous Gard over the tops of oaks
Before him; and while he stared at their appearance,
A cold familiar fear of the unreal
Seized him and held him fixed, like one awaiting
Some blast of magic that would shake them down
To dust, and all within them, and Isolt.
He saw the night-like hair and the white arms
And the wet-shining eyes that half asleep
Had laughed at him again before he left them,
Still shining and still sleepy; and for the while
He saw them, he saw neither towers nor walls;

[153]

And for a moment while he could see nothing,
He was not large enough to hold his heart.
But soon he smiled, seeing where nothing yet
Had crashed or vanished, or was like to fail him,
And moved along slowly around the place
To a green field that like a sea of land
Lay flecked and shadowed by the summer wind
That swept it, saying nothing of how soon
Or late the trampling feet of men and horses
Would make a sorry shambles of it all,
And for another queen.   He wandered on,
And the green grass was music as he walked—
Until beyond it there were trees again,
And through them was the sea, still silver-white,
And flashing as before.   Wherever he looked,
He saw dark eyes and hair and a white face
That was not white, but was the color of love;
Or that was near enough to being a name,
He thought—or might have thought, had he been thinking—
For that which had no name.   To think at all
Would be a more perfidious insolence
To fate, he felt, than to forget the sun
That shone this morning down on Joyous Gard,

Where now there was all joy. He felt it shining,
And throughout time and space he felt it singing;
He felt and heard it moving on the grass
Behind him, and among the moving trees
Around him, and along the foaming shore,
And in the ocean where he splashed and swam
Like a triumphant and almighty fish,
Relinquishing the last concern of earth,
Save one that followed him. Below the waves
There were dark laughing eyes and faintly seen
Phantasmal flashings and white witcheries,
Like those of a dim nixie to be trusted
Never to drown him, or not willingly,
Nor to deceive him. For the time it takes
For joy to think of death and to forget it,
He thought of himself drowned. But when his head
Came up and above water, and he was blind
At first with many a shaft of laughing fire,
All shot from somewhere out of violet eyes,
He had thought long enough. Some day or other
He might think more of it, but for some time
He was to live not thinking of his end,
Or thinking of it he was not to live.

On shore again, he wished all mortal choice,
If choice there was, might come only to that.
Whatever it was that filled life high and full,
It was not time. So he had told Isolt
Under the stars; and so he told himself
Under the trees, and was believing it
With all his might and main. Something on him
Had fallen, in all appearance, that fell not
On men that for one reason or another
Were to fill life with time. He stretched his arms.
Laughing to be alive; and over his head
Leaves in the wind that gave them a gay voice
Flickered and ticked with laughter, saying to him,
"Tristram, it is for you to stay or go.
You will not go. If you leave all there is
That fate calls yours—one jewel of a lustre
More than of earth and of all else on earth,
Glowing in more than gold—the gods that live
In trees will tell the others, and there shall be
No place prepared in heaven or hell for one
Who failed in seeing until too late to see,
That for the sake of living it was his life
And all there was of life that he was leaving.

Probably you will not live very long
If you stay here; and the gods who live in trees
Care little how long man lives." He laughed again
To think of that, and heard the leaves and waves
Laughing to think of that. Like a man lost
In paradise, and before his time to die,
He wandered inland, much at ease with fate,
And in precarious content secure.

Security, the friendly mask of change
At which we smile, not seeing what smiles behind it.
For days and nights, and for more days and nights,
And so for more and more, was unmolested
Through a long vigil over Joyous Gard;
And no dark thunder coming from the west,
Or lightning, shook security, or seared it,
Or touched those walls and towers with even a flick
Significant of irruption or invasion.
He who had laughed at what the laughing trees
Had said, may have laughed well.

                              Summer was going,
When one day Tristram, having heard pleasantly

Isolt's half-hearted and by now less frequent
Reversion to the inveterate whether or not
Of her deserting him in time to save him,
Or of his vanishing, said, stroking her
As if she were some admirable cat,
"Whenever I set myself to count the pounds
Of beauty you have for your not having them,—
Through fear for me, perhaps,—I could affirm
That your disturbance has a virtue in it,
Which I had not foreseen.   Were you too happy,
Your face might round itself like a full fruit,
And all those evanescent little planes
And changes that are like celestial traps
To catch and hold and lose the flying lights
And unseen shadows that make loveliness,
Might go—or rather might not be left the same;
Although if I saw you deformed and twisted,
You would still be the same."

                              "Dear child of thought,
Who forgets nothing if we give him time,"
She said, "if you saw me deformed and twisted,
You might sail back to Brittany so fast

That all the little fishes would be frightened.
Never persuade yourself that you believe
Or need believe, so boundlessly as that.
You will be happier if you leave to me
The love of someone else's imperfections.
I know—but never mind that. It will not come.
We are not for the fireside, or for old age
In any retreat of ancient stateliness.
If that were so, then this would not be so.
Yet when this fragment of your longer life
Has come and gone, it will have come and gone.
There is no doubt of that; and unseen years
May tell your memory more of me than love
May let you know today. After those years
In Cornwall, where my fire of life burned lower
Than you have ever known, I can say this.
Mine is a light that will go out sometime,
Tristram. I am not going to be old.
There is a little watchman in my heart
Who is always telling me what time it is.
I'll say this once to you, and never but once,
To tell you better why harm, for my poor sake,
Must not be yours. I could believe it best—

If I could say it—to say it was all over.
There is your world outside, all fame and banners,
And it was never mine to take from you.
You must not let me take your world away
From you, after all this.   Love is not that.
Before you are much older, I suppose
You will go back to Brittany, where Isolt—
That other Isolt—will think, and some day know.
Women are not so bitter if once they know,
And if the other is dead.   Now forget that,
And kiss me as if we were to live for ever.
Perhaps we shall, somewhere."

                         She smiled at him
And shivered, and they were silent for a while.
Then she said, "Do not say it.   You'll only say
That if I lost my ears and had no hair,
And I had whelks and moles all over my face,
Your love would be the same as it is now—
So let's believe, and leave it.   And if not that,
Your love would find new benefits and rewards
In losing all for me—while yet there's time
Not to lose all.   If you think only of me,

You may forget how far a king's arm reaches,
And what reprisals he may buy with gold
And golden promises."

                        "May the kings all
Be damned," he said, "and their reprisals also.
If this that you have hidden from me so well
Hides truth within it—and may God say no!—
I shall have one more right, if more be needed,
Never to let you go while I'm alive.
Tell me you said it only to be sure
There was no truth in it."

                        She said no more,
And only smiled again, shaking her head,
While in her calm and shining eyes he found
Another last look; and it was not like one
That he had seen before and had remembered
Ever since that cold moonlight on those stairs,
And those cold waves below. But though the way
She looked at him this time, and all she told
So silently, and all she did not tell,
Was not forgotten, security remained

Unchanging, and a friendly sentinel;
And neither, as with a hush of understanding,
Save with unwilling eyes now and again,
Said more of shadows; and while autumn came,
Tristram would see no cloud, or a cloud coming,
Between them and the sun. Whether it rained
Or not, the sun was always shining there,
Or wheresoever the hour might find him riding,
Or sailing home with singing fishermen,
Or losing himself in forage of new scenes,
Alone, for the sheer joy of being alone
And seeing Isolt behind him with Brangwaine
And Gouvernail, and with almost a town
Of Lancelot's men and women to attend them.

Love must have wings to fly away from love,
And to fly back again. So Tristram's love,
And Tristram with it, flew, for the sake of flying,
Far as it would; and if he fared alone
Through mist and rain, there were two violet eyes
That made of mist and rain a pleasant fire,
Warming him as he went. If on the sea
That fell and rose interminably around him,

[162]

His manful avocation was to feign
Escape from blue-black waves of Irish hair,
There were no other waves worth mentioning.
And if allured by unfamiliar scenes
And distances, he found himself astray,
Or comfortably lost, there was no red
That any western sky might show so fair
Beyond the world as one that was still on it,
A red that mixed itself alive with white,
Never the same way twice. It mantled now
Fairer than phantom flame in a white face
That was itself a phantom, and yet so real
That seeing it fade and smile and fade again,
He trembled, wondering still and still assured
That not far off, and always waiting for him
In Joyous Gard, while he saw pictures of her
That were almost Isolt alive to see,
There was Isolt alive that he could feel
When his hands touched her, and find musical
When his heart listened. There were other women
Who murmured peradventure for men's ears
To hear, yet while his own were not engaged
Or implicated they were ghosts of women,

Dumb in a hell of men that had no ears,
For all they were to him—albeit his love
Of everything, where everything was Isolt,
Would not have had that so.

                                    Having outwalked
His hours, he yielded to the setting sun,
And soon enhancing for the eyes of man
With gold of earth, and with his exaltation,
The distant gold of heaven, he borrowed a horse
For a journey, never alone, through falling shadows
And falling leaves.   Back to the walls and towers
He went that now held heaven and all but God
To welcome him with wild and happy eyes
And dark hair waving over them, and a flame
Of red that in the firelight was immersed
In burning white, white fire and red together,
And her white arms to hold him while she asked
Where he had been, what insects he had seen,
And who was king of Salem.   Leaves and flowers,
Wild roses for Isolt, encumbered him,
But were no bulk or burden as on he rode,
Singing, and seeing always in the firelight

He should find shining at his journey's end—
Isolt, always Isolt. She was not there,
He fancied, smiling; she had never been there,
Save in a dream of his; the towers and walls
Of Joyous Gard were only a dream of his;
But heaven had let him dream for a whole summer,
And he was dreaming still as he rode through
The silent gate, where there were silent men
Who looked at him as if he were a stranger,
Whose tongue was none of theirs. Troubled and vexed,
He felt the stillness of a difference
In their attention, as for some defect
Or lapse of his that he could not remember;
And saying a word about a stranger's horse,
He passed them on his way to the still door
Where joy so often entered and came out.
A wonted sense of welcome failing him,
He summoned it from the twilight on the stairs
And half began to sing with a dry throat
That held no song. He entered the same room
Where first Isolt had found him waiting for her,
And where, since then, he had so often found
Isolt, waiting for him. She was not there—

And that was strange. She was not always there,
But it was strange that she was not there now.
He stared about him, wondering that one room,
Holding so many things that he had seen,
And seen again, should hold at the same time
So much of silence. What had happened there?
Where were those arms, and the dark happy eyes,
Always half wet with joy at sight of him?
He made himself insist that he could smile
While helpless drops of fear came out of him,
And he asked of his heart that beat so hard
Why he should be afraid. It was no mark
In his experience to be found afraid,
But he could find no name warmer than fear
For the cold sickness that was in him now,
Although he named it only to disown it.
"A woman may not be always in one place,"
He thought, and said, "Isolt!" She was not there.
He saw the chimney, and saw no fire was there—
And that was strange. It was not always there,
But there or not there, it should be there now.
"And all fires are not lighted at one time,"
He thought, and said, "Isolt!" There was no sound

In this room, or the next room, or the next;
There was no sound anywhere in the whole house—
Except the pounding of his heart, which felt
To him as if it were the whole of him.
He was afraid, and done with all disowning,
And perilously was not afraid of that.
"Is not one here who dares to answer me?"
He muttered slowly, but he could not move—
Not even when he believed that he heard something
Alive behind the heavy velvet curtain
Where he had heard Isolt, so long ago
That now it seemed that she might never have come,
If now she were not gone. For a gasp of time
That only fooled him to a surer knowing
That this was not Isolt, he told himself
It was—-like a man dying who lies to life
For the last empty joy of a last lie.
The sound he heard was not the mouse-like noise
That mice and women make. Be what it might,
He scarcely heard it; and not heeding it,
He stood alone with his hands hanging clenched,
More like a man of bronze than a man breathing,
Until he shook and would have swayed and fallen

Had he not stumbled heavily to a couch
That filled a corner filled already with shadows.
Sitting inert upon the edge of it,
He sent a searching gaze all over the room,
Seeing everything but the one thing he strove
To see; and last he stared upon the floor
Before him, where lay scattered some wild flowers.
Wild roses for Isolt, and saw them there
As if they were a thousand miles away.
Then he looked up again, turning his face
Enough to see in the same room with him,
Rigid and silent, like a friend ordained
To strike again a friend already stricken,
Gawaine from Camelot. Tristram arose,
Propping himself with pride and courtesy,
And stood there waiting for Gawaine to tell him
As much as he might tell.

                  "I have come too late."
He said; and then the look of Tristram vanquished
And routed the battalion of brave words
That he had mustered. "And for that I'm sorry.
Mark is abroad again, and has been free

For just how long the aevil himself may know.
The Queen was by the shore, under some trees,
Where she would sit for hours alone sometimes,
Watching the ocean—or so Brangwaine says—
Alone and happy. Your wits will see the rest.
They carried her off with them in a small boat,
And now she's on a ship that sails to Cornwall.
I do not know a land that has a law
Whereby a man may follow a king's ship
For the king's wife, and have a form of welcome
Better than battle. You are not trimmed for that.
Forgive me—we did all we could. I am here,
And here too late. If I were you, I fancy,
I should tear one more leaf out of my book,
And let the next new page be its own story."

Each word of Gawaine's, falling like a blow
Dealt viciously by one unseen, fell slowly,
And with a not premeditated aim,
So accurate and unfailing in its proof
That when the last had fallen—without reply,
And without time to summon will or reason,
Tristram, the loud accredited strong warrior,

[169]

Tristram, the learned Nimrod among hunters,
Tristram, the loved of women, the harp-player,
Tristram, the doom of his prophetic mother,
Dropped like a log; and silent on the floor,
With wild flowers lying around him on the floor—
Wild roses for Isolt—lay like a log.

Gawaine, Brangwaine, and Gouvernail all waited
By the couch where they had laid him, but no words
Of any resigned allegiance to a fate
That ruled all men acknowledging its rewards,
And its ingratitudes and visitations,
Were on his tongue to say; and in his eyes
There was no kind of light that any one there
Had seen in them before. After long time,
He stared at Brangwaine, and his lips moved once,
Trying to speak, but he said nothing then;
And he said nothing that was heard that night
By man or woman.

There was a week gone by
When Gawaine, less obscured at each day's end
In his confusions, and far less at home
Than ever, saw fit to feel that his return

Was urging him away. His presence there
Was no contagious good that he could see,
And he felt lonely and unnecessary.
There was no Tristram left that he remembered;
Brangwaine, whenever she saw him, did not see him;
And Gouvernail, to one who had always lived
For life, was only gloom looking for death,
And no right company for Gawaine. Brangwaine,
He learned, was going away with him tomorrow,
As far as Camelot, and he sighed to say so,
Seeing how fair she was. "Brangwaine, Gawaine, . . .
A deal of music in this world is wasted,"
He thought, "because a woman cries and kills it.
They've taken away Isolt, Tristram is mad,
Or dead, or God knows what's the name of it,
And all because a woman had eyes and ears,
And beauty enough to strike him dumb with it.
Why must a man, where there are loaves and fishes,
See only as far as one crumb on his table?
Why must he make one morsel of a lifetime?
Here is no place for me. If this be love,
May I live all alone out on a rock,
And starve out there with only the sea to drink,

[171]

And only myself to eat. If this be love,
May I wear blinkers always, or better yet,
Go blindfold through the perils of this world,
Which I have always liked, and so, God help me,
Be led to safety like a hooded horse
Through sparks and unseen fire. If this be love,
May I grow merry and old and amiable
On hate. I'll fix on someone who admires me,
And sting him, and then hate him all my days.
'Gawaine, Brangwaine,' —what else is that than song?
If I were a musician, and had leisure,
I'd surely some day make a tune of it.
'Brangwaine, Gawaine.' " He frowned upon events,
And sighed again that men were not alike.
" 'Gawaine, Brangwaine,' " Brangwaine was fair to see,
And life, while he could sing, was not very long,
And woe not his annoyed him.

                              Gawaine went
With all his men, and Brangwaine, the next day;
And Tristram, like a statue that was moving,
Still haunted Joyous Gard, where Gouvernail,
Disconsolate, and half scared out of sorrow,
Followed and feared, and waited for a sound

Of more than Yes or No. So for a month
He waited, hearing nothing of life without,
Barring a word from Camelot of Isolt
In Cornwall, and alive. He told Tristram,
And Tristram said, "Alive!" Saying no more,
He watched the waves with eyes where Gouvernail
Saw not what he would see in them. The light
That had been Tristram was gone out of them,
And Tristram was not there, even when he spoke,
Saying at last, "This is not good for you,
Gouvernail. You are not my friend for this.
Go back to Brittany and forget all this."
Gouvernail's ears were glad and his heart danced
To hear so many words, but long days passed
And went before he heard so many again.
Then came a letter which a stranger brought,
Who, seeing it held by Tristram, rode away,
Saying his work was done. With avid hands
And eyes half blind with hope, he tore it open,
To make whatever he would of words like these:

"Greeting, Sir Tristram, Prince of Lyonesse.
It was a joy to share with you a house

Where I was once. That was a pleasant house,
Say what you will of it; and it was pleasant
Of me to make you safe and comfortable,
Say what you will of that. This will be sent
For your distinguished and abused attention
From my domain, here in this land of Gore,
Which is my land, and is a pleasant land.
As you may say of it yourself sometime.
More to the salt and essence, there's a lady
Alive in Cornwall—or she was alive—
Who is alone and sore bestead, I fear me,
Amort for love of you. If you go soon—
Too soon you cannot go, if you would see her—
And are not burned alive, or flayed alive,
Or otherwise hindered or invalidated,
You may behold once more that Irish hair,
And those same Irish eyes that once engaged
And occupied you to your desperation.
I cannot answer on more authority
Than hope for your reception or return,
But you, being orgulous and full as an egg
Of fate, may find a way through fire and steel
To see that face again. Were I a man,

And were I thus apprised as to the lady,
I should anon be rowelling my good horse,
And on my way to Cornwall.   Peace be with you,
And may no evil await or overtake you.
Farewell, Sir Tristram, Prince of Lyonesse."

Too sorely stricken already to feel stings,
Tristram, with Morgan's letter crushed and wrinkled,
Sat unresponsive, seeing, wherever he gazed,
Foam breaking, and dark stairs, and two dark eyes,
Frightened and wild again as when they left him
That night when he left them.   When he would see
No more of them, he said to Gouvernail,
"Tomorrow I shall go for a far journey,
And may go farther still.   So, Gouvernail,
Go back to Brittany and forget all this,
And tell them there that they were not forgotten.
Nothing that I can send or say to her
Will do much good.   And if I lied to her,
She might remember me—only for that.
Tell her that I meant always to be kind—
And that's a little to tell.   Say there was more
Than I was, or am yet, to be between us—
And that's a little to say to her.   But say it."

"Sometime I will, Tristram, but not tomorrow.
Tomorrow I go with you, unless you kill me,"
Gouvernail said, "and that would be a little
For you to do. I have seen in and out,
And I'm as wise today as when my mother
Was glad because I cried that I was born.
Your mother was not, you say.   Well, perhaps not."

IX

Against a parapet that overlooked
The sea, lying now like sound that was asleep,
King Mark sat gazing at Isolt's white face,
Mantled no more with red, and pale no longer
With life. The poor dominion that was his
Of her frail body was not revenge enough
To keep even hate alive, or to feed fury.
There was a needlessness about it now
That fury had not foreseen, and that foresight
Would never have forestalled.   The sight of her
Brought back to him a prisoner by his men
From Joyous Gard, and her first look at him,
Had given to death a smallness, and to life,
Ready for death, an uncomplaining triumph

Like nothing of his.   There might be Tristram dead
By stealth, yet there would always be that face—
Isolt's white face.   He saw it now, and said,
"I am not looking to you for much regard,
Though you might let your eyes, if not your tongue,
Say where I am.   Do they know that I am here?
Why are you looking at the sea so long?"

"The sea was never so still as this before,"
She said.   "It is like something after life,
And it is not like death.   That ship out there
Is like two ships, and one of them a shadow.
When you came, I was asking if the shadow
Might not, if only we knew shadows better,
Be the real ship.   I am not very well;
And lately I've had fancies.   Do not mind them.
I have never seen the sea so still as this."

"Perhaps the sea is like ourselves," Mark said,
"And has as much to say of storms and calms
That shake or make it still, as we have power
To shake or to be still.   I do not know.
I was just saying it for no harm or reason.
I shall do no more harm to either of you

Hereafter, and cannot do more to myself.
I should have lost my nature not to take you
Away from him—but now, having you here,
I'm not so sure of nature as once I was.
If it were fate for man here to be sure,
He might not stay so long. I do not know.
All I know now is that you sent for me,
And that I've told you all, or I believe so,
That you would hear me say. A month ago,
He might have stepped from folly to sure death,
Had his blind feet found Cornwall. But not now.
Your gates and doors are open. All I ask
Is that I shall not see him."

                      Isolt said then,
"There was a time when I should have told God
Himself that he had made you without mercy.
Forgive me that. For there was your side, always;
There were your ways, which are the ways of kings;
And there was blindness everywhere at first—
When there was all that time! You are kind now,
And I thank God that you are merciful."
"When there is nothing left for us to lose,

There's no great mercy in our not losing it,"
He said. "God will not hear you if you thank him
Only for that. A weary spark of sense,
Or a dull feel of reason, is not mercy.
I have not changed. I'm only some days older
Than when they brought you back from there—brought you
And your white face together. You looked at me,
And I saw your white face."

                She smiled at him,
And touched his hand with hers: "You are good to me.
Whatever you do, I shall not be here long.
Whatever you are, you have been good to me.
I shall not be afraid of you again—
No, nor of Andred. When he knows of this,
He will bow down to your authority
Like a small hungry dog and lick your fingers.
And all his insane hatred for Tristram,
And all his worse than insane love for me . . .
Poor loveless atom!"

              "Andred?" Mark said. scowling
And went on with a hoarse unhappy laugh:
"Morgan, when she was here, was playing with him

So much like a damned cat that I believed
His love, if you say love, was all for her.
I wondered that she wasted so much guile
Upon so little grace. The fellow is mad.
I should have seen that he was always mad.
We were all mad—that night. I should have seen.
I should have seen . . ." He rose and stalked along
Before the parapet, and back again;
Then, with a groan that savored of a snarl,
He cried, "God knows what else I should have seen!
Had I been made with eyes to read in the dark
All that was written there, I might have seen,
By straining them, some such effect as this.
How could I see where there was nothing shown
Or told for me to see? There was yourself,
But I believed that home was in your eyes,
Rather than hate, and that a crown to wear
Would outshine all your tears. Had I known early
All that I knew too late . . . I do not know.
I am not sure."

        "Whether you are or are not,"
She said, "you have been kind to me today.
You will not live, though you should live for ever,
[180]

To wish this kindness back. You might have given
Me nothing, and I should not have wondered more
Than I have wondered at your giving me this.
I should have suffered, and not thought it strange.
There was a cloud that covered us all, and now
You have been kind. If it was fate, we'll say
Bad fate was like bad weather. Oh, it is hard,
With such a stillness lying on everything
Today, to say that storms have ever been."

"There have been storms enough to sink us all,
And drown us. Yet we are still here afloat—
Here, or somewhere. Not even that ship you see
Will be there always."

                    "And ships in their last port,"
She said, "have still a farther voyage to make,
Wherever it is they go. Were it not for love,
Poor life would be a ship not worth a launching.
Is it not true?"

            "I do not know," Mark said;
And for a long time stared upon the sea,
Which told him nothing.

Isolt, watching him there,
And with a furtive sorrow in her heart
For one that was foredoomed to be himself,
Felt presently the coming of quick feet
Up the stone stairs within the walls behind her;
And turning where she lay, saw Brangwaine's fingers
Upon her lips, and saw more in her eyes
Than joy alone, or fear. Only one thing
Was there in life remaining to mean either;
And the wild red came back to Isolt's cheeks,
And to her throat.

"He is waiting," Brangwaine said,
"And has the manner, if I may dare to say so,
Of one who should not wait."

"Why should he wait?"
Mark answered, with a sullen glance at her;
And then, after one long unhappy look
At where Isolt was lying—or now half lying—
Went through the doorway and led Brangwaine with him,
Leaving Isolt alone to watch the sea
Until there was no sea, and she saw nothing—

Not even when she felt arms shaking that held her,
And his lips, after so long, on hers again,
And on her cheeks and eyes. When she could see,
She shrank a little away from him for love
And wonder, and then for love and fear she drew
His face down to her heart and held it there
While her heart ached and it seemed right to die.
Searching his eyes to find him, she said only,
"I shall hear all you do not say to me,
Tristram. For you are only one man still,
Which is a thing that one man may forget.
You forget rest."

                    "I shall remember it—
Sometime," he said. "When rest remembers me,
There will be time for that. I shall have rest."
Then he sat still, holding her hands as lightly
As if they were two leaves, and stared at her
Like a man back from death. "What has Mark done
That I should find his doors all open for me,
And see no swords, or fire? You have done this.
There is no other woman, and no man,
To do it. I can see now. The king of hell

Would not refuse, if your eyes asked him now,
To open the doors of hell."

                    "They are all open,
Tristram, and I shall not go out of them—
Or I shall not go out as I came in.
They are the doors of heaven while you are here,
And shall be so when you are gone from here;
For I shall keep you here.   Mark, I suppose,
Knew that.   Mark has been good to me today—
So good that I might almost think him sorry
That he is Mark, and must be always Mark.
May we be sorry to be ourselves, I wonder?
I am not so, Tristram.   You are not so.
Is there much then to sigh for?"

                    "I am not sighing
For that," he said, and kissed her thin white fingers.
"My love will tell you, if you need be told
At all, why sorrow comes with me . . . Isolt!
Isolt!"

          She smiled.   "I am not afraid to die,
Tristram, if you are trying to think of that—

Or not to think of that.   Why think of it?
My cup was running over; and having had all
That one life holds of joy, and in one summer,
Why should I be a miser crying to God
For more?   There was a way for this to be,
And this must be the way.   There was no other;
And I would have no other—not for myself.
Not now.   Not now.   It is for you, Tristram,
That I see this way best."

                    "God knows," he said,
"How well my love, which is the best of me,
Knows what a gulf of trust and understanding
There is in yours, where I would drown and die
So gladly and so soon, could I, by going
That way, leave you behind me here, and happy.
I would be gone from you and be forgotten
Like waves in childhood on forgotten water,
If that were the way left to bring warm life
And warm joy back into these cheeks again,
And these eyes looking at me."

                    The eyes smiled,
And the cheeks flushed with gladness; and Isolt

Said without sorrow, "I would not give two grains
Of sand to stay alive with you forgotten.
But I would give myself, or as much of me
As there is now, for God's word that my love
May not make yours a burden to be borne
Till you be weary of it. If we had seen,
If we had known—when there was all that time!
But no, there's nothing in that. We have known since then
All that we know today. Was it enough?
How shall we measure and weigh these lives of ours?
You said once that whatever it is that fills
Life up, and fills it full, it is not time.
You told my story when you said that to me,
But what of yours? Was it enough, Tristram?
Was it enough to fly so far away
From time that for a season time forgot us?
You said so, once. Was it too much to say?"

Her words had in their pleading an unwilling
And wistful intimation of things ended
That sorrow let escape. But he only smiled,
And pressed her asking hands. "It was enough,"
He said; "and I may tell you more than that,
[186]

Perhaps, when I am God, making new stars
To shine for you to see. They are more than fire,
You said; and they will tell you everything
That I may not say now."

                                "It was enough!"
She murmured; and her words held happiness
Heard beyond earth, he thought. He turned his eyes
Away from hers that closed in weariness
And peace, to leave her smiling. Never before
Had such a stillness fallen on land or sea
That he remembered. Only one silent ship
Was moving, if it moved. He turned again
To the low couch before him and saw shining,
Under the darkness of her waving hair,
And with a pallid loveliness not pale
With life around them, the same violet eyes
Fixed upon his and with a calm that hurt him,
Telling him what they told, and holding more
Than it was good to tell. But they could smile
And lie for kindness; and she could tell him lies
While he for kindness listened:

                            "You will go back
To Brittany after this, and there Isolt—

That other Isolt—" she said, "will, as time goes,
Fill up the strange and empty little place
That I may leave; and as time goes, and goes,
You may be king with her across the water;
Or, if you choose, you will be king, may be,
In your land, Lyonesse. I have never known
A man before with kingdoms at his feet,
Like scattered gold for him to leave or take,
And as he will. You will go back again
To Brittany; and when you are an old man,
You will remember this—this afternoon.
I am so sure of it that I'll not ask you
To tell me more about it." Her white fingers
Closed upon his, and her eyes closed again.

"I shall go back to Brittany, sometime,"
He said, "for whatsoever awaits me there.
There may be nothing. Women have changed before:
And more of them would be more fortunate,
For all I know, if more of them might change."

"I have seen many," she said, "like silent birds
Who could not fly with wings they thought were broken.

They were not broken, and the birds did fly.
I have seen wings that have been healed and mended,
Also. I have not seen many of them, perhaps.
Wings are but once for most of those who fly
Till they see time lying under them like a mist
That covers the earth. We have had wings and flown,
And one of us comes to earth again, and time,
Not to find much time left; and that is best
For her. One will have wings to fly again;
And that is best for him."

He looked across
The windless water and forgot what land
It was that lay beyond where he was looking.
He forgot everything, save all there was
For him, and turned again to see it there, lying
So silent, and unendurably so soon
Not to be there; to be so fair there now,
And then to vanish; to be so dark and white
And violet, and to die. And that was best,
She said; and she must know. He heard her saying
And saying again to him that it was best.
She would be saying it all his life to him,

To make him sure, leaving him and his wings
To fly wherever they would. "You do not say
How far I shall be flying, or for how long,"
He told her then, "and that's as well for me.
As for the best, I know no more of that
Than I see in your face and in your love
That looks at me. Love, it was far from here
And far from England and this inchmeal world
That our wings lifted us to let us fly
Where time forgot us. He waited for us here,
But his wings were too old to follow us.
We shall not go so far away from here
Again, till we go farther. It is enough
For me that you should ask if it was so,
And ask it with these eyes."

                              "I would to God
That we might fly together away from here,
Like two birds over the sea," she murmured then,
And her words sang to him. "The sea was never
So still as it is now, and the wind never
So dead. It is like dying, and not like death.
No, do not say things now. This is not you,

Tristram.   There was a mercy in fate for you
That later will be clear, when you see better
Than you need see today.   Only remember
That all there was of me was always yours.
There was no more of me.   Was it enough?
Tell me, was it enough?   You said it was,
And I have still to ask.   Women have ears
That will hold love as deserts will hold rain,
But you have told Isolt it was enough,
And she knows all there is.   When first we met
In darkness, and were groping there together,
Not seeing ourselves—and there was all that time—
She was all yours.   But time has died since then,
Time and the world, and she is always yours.
Pray God she be no burden.   You that are still
To fly, pray God for that."

                              He raised his eyes
And found hers waiting for them.   "Time is not life—
For me," he said.   "But your life was for you.
It was not mine to take away from you."
He went on wanderingly, and his words ached
Like slaves feeling a lash: "It was not mine.

I should have let you go away from there.
I should have made you go, or should have gone
Myself, leaving you there to tell yourself
It was your fear for me that frightened me,
And made me go."

                    "If you should hear my ghost
Laughing at you sometime, you will know why,
Tristram," she said. And over her calm eyes
A smile of pity passed like a small cloud
Over two pools of violet in warm white,
Pallid with change and pain. "It was your life,
For mine was nothing alone. It was not time,
For you or me, when we were there together.
It was too much like always to be time.
If you said anything, love, you said it only
Because you are afraid to see me die—
Which is so little, now. There was no more;
And when I knew that I was here again,
I knew there was no more. . . . It was enough,
And it was all there was."

                    Once more she drew him
Closer, and held him; and once more his head

Was lying upon her with her arms around it
As they would hold a child. She felt the strength
Of a man shaking in his helplessness,
And would not see it. Lying with eyes closed
And all her senses tired with pain and love,
And pity for love that was to die, she saw him
More as a thunder-stricken tower of life
Brought down by fire, than as a stricken man
Brought down by fate, and always to wear scars
That in his eyes and voice were changelessly
Revealed and hidden. There was another voice,
Telling of when there should be left for him
No place among the living any longer;
And there was peace and wisdom, saying to her.
It will be best then, when it is all done.
But her own peace and wisdom frightened her,
And she would see him only as he had been
Before. That was the best for her to see;
And it was best that each should see the other
Unseen, and as they were before the world
Was done with them, and for a little while,
In silence, to forget and to remember.
They did not see the ocean or the sky,

Or the one ship that moved, if it was moving,
Or the still leaves on trees. They did not see
The stairs where they had stood once in the moonlight,
Before the moon went out and Tristram went
From her to darkness, into time and rain,
Leaving her there with Mark and the cold sound
Of waves that foamed all night. They did not see
The silent shore below, or the black rocks,
Or the black shadow of fate that came unfelt,
Or, following it, like evil dressed as man,
A shape that crept and crawled along to Tristram,
And leapt upon him with a shining knife
That ceased to shine. After one cry to God,
And her last cry, she could hear Tristram, saying,
"If it was Andred—give him thanks—for me. . . .
It was not Mark. . . . Isolt!"

                              She heard no more.
There was no more for either of them to hear,
Or tell. It was all done. So there they lay,
And her white arms around his head still held him.
Closer than life. They did not hear the sound
Of Andred laughing, and they did not hear

[194]

The cry of Brangwaine, who had seen, too late,
Andred ascending stealthily alone,
Like death, and with death shining in his hand,
And in his eyes. They did not hear the steps
Of Mark, who followed, or of Gouvernail,
Who followed Mark.

              They were all silent there
While Mark, nearer the couch and watching it,
And all that there was on it, and half on it,
Was unaware of Andred at his knees,
Until he seized them and stared up at him
With unclean gleaming eyes. "Tell me, my lord
And master," he crooned, with fawning confidence,
"Tell me—and say if I have not done well!
See him—and say if I'm a lizard now!
See him, my master! Have I not done well?"

Mark, for a time withheld in angry wonder
At what he saw, and with accusing sorrow
For what he felt, said nothing and did nothing,
Till at the sight of Andred's upturned face
He reached and seized him, saying no word at all,

And like a still machine with hands began
Slowly to strangle him. Then, with a curse,
He flung him half alive upon the floor,
Where now, for the first time, a knife was lying,
All wet with Tristram's blood. He stared at it,
Almost as if his hands had left it there;
And having seen all he would of it, he flung it
Over the parapet and into the sea;
And where it fell, the faint sound of a splash
Far down was the one sound the sea had made
That afternoon. Only the ship had moved—
And was a smaller ship, farther away.
He watched it for a long time, silently,
And then stood watching Tristram and Isolt,
Who made no sound. "I do not know," he said,
And gazed away again from everything.

"No sea was ever so still as this before,"
Gouvernail said, at last; and while he spoke
His eyes were on the two that were together
Where they were lying as silent as the sea.
"They will not ask me why it is not strange
Of me to say so little."

                    "No," Mark answered,
"Nothing was ever so still as this before. . . .
She said it was like something after life,
And it was not like death. She may have meant
To say to me it was like this; and this
Is peace."

                    To make his wonder sure again
That they were there, he looked; and they were there,
And there was Andred, helpless on the floor,
Staring in a mad ecstasy of hope
At Mark, who scanned him with an absent hate
Of nature, and with a doubt—as he had looked
Sometimes at unreal creatures of the sea
Thrown ashore dead by storms. Saying unheard,
With lips that moved as in a tortured sleep,
Words that were only for the dead to hear,
He watched again as he had watched before
The two that were so still where they were lying,
And wondered if they listened—they were so still
Where they were lying. "I do not know," he said,
"What this is you have done. I am not sure . . ."
His words broke slowly of their own heaviness,

And were like words not spoken to be heard:
"I am not sure that you have not done well.
God knows what you have done. I do not know.
There was no more for them—and this is peace."

X

By the same parapet that overlooked
The same sea, lying like sound now that was dead,
Mark sat alone, watching an unknown ship
That without motion moved from hour to hour.
Farther away. There was no other thing
Anywhere that was not as fixed and still
As two that were now safe within the walls
Below him, and like two that were asleep.
"There was no more for them," he said again,
To himself, or to the ship, "and this is peace.
I should have never praise or thanks of them
If power were mine and I should waken them;
And what might once have been if I had known
Before—I do not know. So men will say
In darkness, after daylight that was darkness,
Till the world ends and there are no more kings
And men to say it. If I were the world's maker,

I should say fate was mightier than I was,
Who made these two that are so silent now,
And for an end like this. Nothing in this
Is love that I have found, nor is it in love
That shall find me. I shall know day from night
Until I die, but there are darknesses
That I am never to know, by day or night;
All which is one more weary thing to learn,
Always too late. There are some ills and evils
Awaiting us that God could not invent;
There are mistakes too monstrous for remorse
To fondle or to dally with, and failures
That only fate's worst fumbling in the dark
Could have arranged so well. And here once more
The scroll of my authority presents
Deficiency and dearth. I do not know
Whether these two that have torn life from time,
Like a death-laden flower out of the earth,
Have failed or won. Many have paid with more
Than death for no such flower. I do not know
How much there was of Morgan in this last
Unhappy work of Andred's, or if now
It matters—when such a sick misshapen grief

May with a motion of one feeble arm
Bring this to pass. There is too much in this
That intimates a more than random issue;
And this is peace—whatever it is for me.
Now it is done, it may be well for them,
And well for me when I have followed them.
I do not know."

                Alone he stood there, watching
The sea and its one ship, until the sea
Became a lonely darkness and the ship
Was gone, as a friend goes. The silent water
Was like another sky where silent stars
Might sleep for ever, and everywhere was peace.
It was a peace too heavy to be endured
Longer by one for whom no peace less heavy
Was coming on earth again. So Mark at last
Went sombrely within, where Gouvernail
And silence wearied him. Move as he might,
Silence was all he found—silence within,
Silence without, dark silence everywhere—
And peace.

            And peace, that lay so heavy and dark
That night on Cornwall, lay as dark that night

On Brittany, where Isolt of the white hands
Sat watching, as Mark had watched, a silent sea
That was all stars and darkness. She was looking
With her gray eyes again, in her old way,
Into the north, and for she knew not what
Tonight. She was not looking for a ship,
And there was no ship coming. Yet there she sat,
And long into the night she sat there, looking
Away into the darkness to the north,
Where there was only darkness, and more stars.
No ship was coming that night to Brittany
From Cornwall. There was time enough for ships;
And when one came at last, with Gouvernail,
Alone, she had seen in him the end of waiting,
Before her father's eyes and his bowed head
Confirmed her sight and sense.

                         King Howel paused,
Like one who shifts a grievous weight he carries,
Hoping always in vain to make it lighter,
And after gazing at the large gray eyes
In the wan face before him, would have spoken,
But no speech came. Dimly from where he was,

Through mist that filled his eyes, he pictured her
More as a white and lovely thing to kill
With words than as a woman who was waiting
For truth already told. "Isolt—my child!"
He faltered, and because he was her father,
His anguish for the blow that he was giving
Felt the blow first for her.

                              "You are so kind
To me, my father," she said softly to him,
"That you will hold behind you now the knife
You bring with you, first having let me see it.
You are too kind. I said then to Gawaine
That he would not come back. Tristram is dead.
So—tell me all there is. I shall not die.
I have died too many times already for that.
I shall not ever die. Where was he, father?"
Her face was whiter and her large gray eyes
Glimmered with tears that waited.

                              He told her then
A tale, by Gouvernail and himself twice-tempered,
Of Tristram on his way to Brittany,
Having seen that other Isolt, by Mark's reprieve,

Only once more before she was to die.
It was an insane sort of kinsman, Andred,
Not Mark, who slew him in a jealous hate;
All which was nebulously true enough
To serve, her father trusted, willing to leave
The rest of it unheard, whatever it was,
For time to bury and melt.   With Tristram dead,
This child of his, with her gray eyes that saw
So much, seeing so far, might one day see
A reason to live without him—which, to him,
Her father, was not so hard as to conceive
A reason for man's once having and leaving her.
That night the King prayed heaven to make her see,
And in the morning found his child asleep—
After a night of tears and stifled words,
They told him.   She had made almost no sound
That whole night; and for many a day to follow
She made almost no sound.

                    One afternoon
Her father found her by the sea, alone,
Where the cold waves that rolled along the sand
Were saying to her unceasingly, "Tristram—
Tristram."   She heard them and was unaware

That they had uttered once another name
For Tristram's ears. She did not know of that,
More than a woman or man today may know
What women or men may hear when someone says
Familiar things forgotten, and did not see
Her father until she turned, hearing him speak:

"Two years ago it was that he came here
To make you his unhappy wife, my child,
Telling you then, and in a thousand ways,
Without the need of language, that his love
Was far from here. His willingness and my wish
Were more to save you then, so I believed,
Than to deceive you. You were not deceived;
And you are as far now from all deception,
Or living need of it. You are not going
On always with a ghost for company,
Until you die. If you do so, my way,
Which cannot be a long way now, may still
Be more than yours. If Tristram were alive,
You would be Tristram's queen, and the world's eyes
And mind would be content, seeing it so.
But he is dead, and you have dreamed too long,

Partly because your dream was partly true—
Which was the worst of all, but yet a dream.
Now it is time for those large solemn eyes
Of yours to open slowly, and to see
Before them, not behind. Tristram is dead,
And you are a king's daughter, fairer than fame
Has told—which are two seeds for you to plant
In your wise little head as in a garden,
Letting me see what grows. We pay for dreams
In waking out of them, and we forget
As much as needs forgetting. I'm not a king
With you; I am a father and a man—
A man not over wise or over foolish,
Who has not long to live, and has one child
To be his life when he is gone from here.
You will be Queen some day, if you will live,
My child, and all you are will shine for me.
You are my life, and I must live in you.
Kings that are marked with nothing else than honor
Are not remembered long."

                    "I shall be Queen
Of Here or There, may be—sometime," she said;
"And as for dreaming, you might hesitate

In shaking me too soon out of my sleep
In which I'm walking. Am I doing so ill
To dream a little, if dreams will help me now?
You are not educating me, my father,
When you would seize too soon, for my improvement,
All that I have. You are the dreamer now.
You are not playing today with the same child
Whose dream amused you once when you supposed
That she was learning wisdom at your knees.
Wisdom was never learned at any knees,
Not even a father's, and that father a king.
If I am wiser now than while I waited
For Tristram coming, knowing that he would come,
I may not wait so long for Tristram going,
For he will never go. I am not one
Who must have everything, yet I must have
My dreams if I must live, for they are mine.
Wisdom is not one word and then another,
Till words are like dry leaves under a tree;
Wisdom is like a dawn that comes up slowly
Out of an unknown ocean."

                    "And goes down
Sometimes," the king said, "into the same ocean.

You live still in the night, and are not ready
For the new dawn. When the dawn comes, my child,
You will forget. No, you will not forget,
But you will change. There are no mortal houses
That are so providently barred and fastened
As to keep change and death from coming in.
Tristram is dead, and change is at your door.
Two years have made you more than two years older,
And you must change."

                  "The dawn has come," she said,
"And wisdom will come with it. If it sinks
Away from me, and into night again—
Then I shall be alone, and I shall die.
But I shall never be all alone—not now;
And I shall know there was a fate more swift
Than yours or mine that hurried him farther on
Than we are yet. I would have been the world
And heaven to Tristram, and was nothing to him;
And that was why the night came down so dark
On me when Tristram died. But there was always
Attending him an almost visible doom
That I see now; and while he moved and looked

As one too mighty and too secure to die,
He was not mingled and equipped to live
Very long. It was not earth in him that burned
Itself to death; and she that died for him
Must have been more than earth. If he had lived,
He would have pitied me and smiled at me,
And he would always have been kind to me—
If he had lived; and I should not have known,
Not even when in his arms, how far away
He was from me. Now, when I cannot sleep,
Thinking of him, I shall know where he is."

King Howel shook his head. "Thank God, my child,
That I was wise enough never to thwart you
When you were never a child. If that was wisdom,
Say on my tomb that I was a wise man."
He laid his hands upon her sun-touched hair,
Which in Gawaine's appraisal had no color
That was a name, and saying no more to her
While he stood looking into her gray eyes,
He smiled, like one with nothing else to do;
And with a backward glance unsatisfied,
He walked away.

Isolt of the white hands,
Isolt with her gray eyes and her white face,
Still gazed across the water to the north
But not now for a ship. Were ships to come,
No fleet of them could hold a golden cargo
That would be worth one agate that was hers—
One toy that he had given her long ago,
And long ago forgotten. Yet there she gazed
Across the water, over the white waves,
Upon a castle that she had never seen,
And would not see, save as a phantom shape
Against a phantom sky. He had been there,

She thought, but not with her. He had died there,
But not for her. He had not thought of her,
Perhaps, and that was strange. He had been all,
And would be always all there was for her,
And he had not come back to her alive,
Not even to go again. It was like that
For women, sometimes, and might be so too often
For women like her. She hoped there were not many
Of them, or many of them to be, not knowing
More about that than about waves and foam,
And white birds everywhere, flying, and flying;

Alone, with her white face and her gray eyes,
She watched them there till even her thoughts were white,
And there was nothing alive but white birds flying,
Flying, and always flying, and still flying,
And the white sunlight flashing on the sea.

DATE DUE

PRINTED IN U.S.A.